Isaiah: The Glory of the Messiah

ISAIAH: The Glory of the Messiah

by

Alfred Martin

and

John A. Martin

MOODY PRESS
CHICAGO

Library of Congress Cataloging in Publication Data

Martin, Alfred, 1916-
Isaiah, the glory of the Messiah.

Bibliography: p. 181
1. Bible. O.T. Isaiah—Commentaries. I. Martin,
John A., 1949-   . II. Title.
    BS1515.3.M27 1983 224'.107 83-761
ISBN 0-8024-0168-6

2 3 4 5 Printing/EB/Year 87 86 85 84

Preface

More than twenty-five years ago I wrote a small book on Isaiah for publication by Moody Press. That book made no pretensions of being an exegetical commentary or even a detailed exposition. All it claimed to be was a "brief elementary survey of Isaiah."

The present work goes a step beyond that by seeking to make available to the student or general reader results of the scholarly efforts of many writers and teachers in a form that will be helpful to someone who does not know Hebrew. It is not intended to be a verse-by-verse exegetical commentary, but aims at a practical exposition of Isaiah through a literal, premillennial, and dispensational approach. For that reason we have thought it desirable to avoid heavy documentation. The selective bibliography will be useful to the student who wishes to probe more intensively.

As in the previous book, mastery of the factual content of Isaiah is emphasized as a foundation for continued study and personal application.

It is a special joy to me to be collaborating in this undertaking with my son, Dr. John A. Martin, assistant professor of Bible exposition, Dallas Theological Seminary, whose major study has been in Old Testament literature and exegesis.

Alfred Martin
Formerly vice-president and dean of education
The Moody Bible Institute of Chicago

Professor of Bible
Dallas Bible College

Contents

CHAPTER   PAGE

Introduction
Impressions of Isaiah 11
Magnitude of the Prophecy 11
The Majesty and Greatness of God 12
The Reality of the Promised Kingdom 13
The Messianic Character of the Book 14
The Nature of Prophecy 15
The Historical Background of Isaiah 17
Place of Isaiah in the Canon 18
The Writer of the Book 19
The Prophet's Name as the Theme 19
The Unity of Isaiah 21
External Evidence 22
Internal Evidence 23
Background of the Critical Views of Isaiah 26
The Use of Isaiah in the New Testament 26
Further Thoughts on Isaiah's Style 27
Basic Outline of the Book 28
Outline of the First Part of Isaiah 30
Analysis of the Second Part of Isaiah 30
Outline of the Second Part of Isaiah 31
1. Opening Prophecies: The Lord's Case Against
  Judah (1:1—6:13) 33
Heading of the Whole Book 34
God's Indictment 36
God's Vengeance 38

Messiah's Reign   39
Appeal and Warning   41
The Branch of the Lord   43
The Song of the Vineyard   43
Isaiah's Call and Commission   44
2. The Book of Immanuel (7:1—12:6)   51
The Birth of Immanuel   52
The Assyrian Invasion   57
The Davidic Kingdom and King   59
God's Stretched-out Hand of Judgment   62
The Branch from Jesse's Roots   63
The Song of Redemption   66
3. The Burdens on the Nations (13:1—23:18)   67
Oracle Concerning Babylon   69
Oracle Concerning Philistia   74
Oracle Concerning Moab   74
Oracle Concerning Damascus   75
Oracle Concerning the Land of Whirring Wings   76
Oracle Concerning Egypt   76
Oracle Concerning the Desert   77
Oracle Concerning Edom   78
Oracle Concerning Arabia   78
Oracle Concerning the Valley of Vision   78
Oracle Concerning Tyre   79
Conclusion of the Burdens   79
4. Punishment Followed by Kingdom Blessing
(24:1—27:13)   81
Troubles Followed by the Reign of the Lord of
Hosts   82
Praise of God for His Wonderful Works   83
A Song of Salvation   83
God's Indignation and the Regathering of Israel   84
5. Pronouncement of Woes (28:1—33:24)   85
Woe to Ephraim   85
Warning to the Rulers of Judah   86
Woe to Jerusalem (Ariel)   87
Woe to the Egyptian Alliance   88
The Righteous King Who Will Deliver   90
Woe to Assyria   91
6. Indignation and Glory (34:1—35:10)   93
The Lord's Indignation   93
The Blossoming Desert   95

7. Historical Interlude (36:1—39:8)   97
   God's Deliverance of Jerusalem from Sennacherib   99
   Hezekiah's Illness and Miraculous Recovery   101
8. Deliverance of God's People (40:1—48:22)   105
   The Comfort of God for Delivered Israel   106
   The Character and Omnipotence of God   108
   Further Proof of the Lord's Power and Deity   110
   The Lord's Servant Who Will Bring Judgment   114
   The Power of God Manifest Through His Servant   115
   Israel's Privilege and Responsibility as God's Servant   116
   The Powerful God and the Powerless Idols   117
   God's Purposes Through Cyrus, His Anointed   119
   Judgment on Babylon's Idols   120
   Judgment on the Babylonian Empire   122
   Exhortations to the Impenitent and Unbelieving   123
9. The Suffering Servant as the Redeemer
   (49:1—57:21)   125
   God's Salvation Through the Servant   125
   Exhortations to the Unbelieving   126
   Exhortations to the Righteous   127
   Zion's Joy in the Lord's Deliverance   129
   The Suffering Servant of the Lord   131
   Restoration of Israel to the Place of Blessing   142
   Appeal to Come to God for Salvation   144
   Moral Exhortations in View of God's Salvation   146
   Contrast of the Contrite and the Wicked   147
10. The Glorious Consummation (58:1—66:24)   151
   Repentance Followed by Blessing   151
   The Coming of the Redeemer to Zion   152
   The Glory of Israel   153
   The Ministry of the Messiah   155
   Jerusalem a Praise in the Earth   161
   The Day of Vengeance   163
   The Prayer of the Remnant   166
   Condemnation and Glory   168
   Peace Like a River   170
Appendix 1: An Inductive Validation of the Central
   Theme of Isaiah   173
Appendix 2: Quotations from Isaiah in the New
   Testament   177
Bibliography   181
Scripture Index   183

Introduction

The book of Isaiah has always been regarded as an especially beautiful literary production. Of course, it is much more than that because it is part of the written Word of God.

One should not compare one part of Scripture with another part to the detriment of either, for it is all the pure, holy, life-giving message from the infinite God, the gracious heavenly Father of all those who put their trust in the Lord Jesus Christ.

Nevertheless, it is permissible and even desirable to note some of the major features that make Isaiah an outstanding book. Each person who reads and studies Isaiah doubtless will have impressions of his own. These are some of the impressions that are common to many readers.

IMPRESSIONS OF ISAIAH

MAGNITUDE OF THE PROPHECY

One such impression is the sheer magnitude of the prophecy. There is so much here in range of time, space, and ideas that even one who is familiar with the book will frequently be overwhelmed. Led by the Spirit of God, the prophet gave a comprehensive view of his own time: a period of turmoil, war, misery, and fear for many of his contemporaries, and yet a time of witness to, service for, and confidence in the sovereign Lord who is the disposer of all events.

Carried along by the Holy Spirit, Isaiah looked ahead to his own country's destruction by the Babylonians, and then beyond that to the return. That return from the Babylonian captivity, however, is not the ultimate in deliverance. It furnishes the prophet with the analogy for looking toward a much greater deliverance in the more distant future—deliverance through the Messiah, who is so prominent in this book.

One cannot stress too much the necessity of reading and meditating on the book of Isaiah itself. Commentaries can be helpful, but they must not get in the way of the inspired text. The way to know Isaiah is to read *Isaiah*—a self-evident truth often overlooked even by some earnest Bible students.

The Word of God is both like and unlike other books. It must be studied, for its contents cannot be acquired in some magical way without effort. Yet there is a spiritual as well as an intellectual element in its apprehension. One could know the various sections of the book perfectly and even think through it chapter by chapter without comprehending its spiritual teaching. Therefore, the careful student will avoid mere knowledge for the sake of knowledge, but he will acquire knowledge as a means to a greater understanding and appreciation of what God has given. One should always allow the Spirit of God to make personal application of Scripture to one's own life.

It is useless to trace the judgment of God in Isaiah and to note God's comfort for His people, and to see how these two elements —judgment and comfort—make a unified whole, if one sees it all only as an abstraction, as a lovely but theoretical essay or story. The Bible is intensely practical, and if one cannot learn from both its precepts and its examples, something must be lacking in the experience of the reader. One must not become so absorbed in the beauties of style and the symmetrical arrangement of Isaiah that one loses sight of his own need of repentance and trust in the Redeemer depicted there.

Nor should one become discouraged if he cannot see immediately all the relationships of the parts to the whole. The book is admittedly overwhelming, but familiarity will help. In contemplating the things of God, familiarity does *not* breed contempt, but rather the opposite. The saint who has made the Scriptures his lifetime study seems to be awed more and more by them.

THE MAJESTY AND GREATNESS OF GOD

A second impression from Isaiah is the realization of the majesty and greatness of God. The God who is described in this book in His omniscience, omnipotence, omnipresence, eternality, immutability, holiness, love, mercy, and grace cannot, by any stretch of the imagination, be brought down to the level of destructive critics. To speak of the God of the Old Testament as a "tribal" or "national" God is sheer nonsense, and it is equally nonsensical to suppose that the godly people of Old Testament times thought of God in any such way. As will be sufficiently demonstrated, Isaiah portrays God as the one and only living and true God who deserves and demands universal acceptance and worship. Isaiah's message is a universal message, reaching to the "ends of the earth."

In the course of this study some of the outstanding names of God in Isaiah will be examined, including His covenant name, YHWH (generally spelled *Yahweh*, or in the older tradition *Jehovah*), as well as Isaiah's distinctive title for God, the "Holy One of Israel." The majesty of God is related to His moral character. As the Holy One, He is not the God of mere naked power, but the God of holiness. His nature is always in perfect harmony with His moral character. All that He is and all that He does is absolutely right, pure, and free from all defilement of sin. Because He is the Holy One, He can redeem those who put their trust in Him and must judge and punish those who reject and disobey Him.

Along with his descriptions of God's glory and majesty and his characterization of God as the Holy One, Isaiah does not neglect the aspect of God's character comprehended in the term *the love of God*. His goodness, longsuffering, mercy, grace, gentleness, and lovingkindness are all seen in abundant measure in the pages of this great prophetic book.

THE REALITY OF THE PROMISED KINGDOM

Another impression gained from the reading of Isaiah is the reality of the promised kingdom for the nation of Israel. In the face of so large a body of prophecy concerning future blessings for the despised and scattered nation, it is hard to see how so many readers and interpreters blithely assume that the church is everywhere in view; that the church is Israel, that the church is the kingdom, and that there is no objective standard in the fulfillment of prophecy. Because of that prevalent misconception, this study places a great amount of stress on the literal fulfillment of prophecy.

THE MESSIANIC CHARACTER OF THE BOOK

Still another impression is the messianic character of the book of Isaiah. It will be developed in a number of places in the commentary, but at this point it is sufficient to say that the faithful reading of Isaiah will reveal why he is so often called the "prophet of the gospel" or the "evangelical prophet." One could construct a fairly detailed account of the earthly life and ministry and the death and resurrection of the Lord Jesus Christ from the pages of Isaiah alone. The messianic references are not confined to one section of the book, but are scattered throughout.

Yet one must not make the mistake made by the religious leaders of Christ's day. They looked for eternal life in the bare pages of Scripture and rejected the Person whom those pages described (see John 5:39-40).

It is not enough to marvel at the prophetic pictures of Christ in Isaiah, pictures so sharply drawn that they could not be accidental. One must have a personal relationship to the Christ described there. The gospel is here in its pure essence, given prophetically by the Holy Spirit long before the Lord Jesus actually came into the world. Isaiah saw His glory (John 12:41), and the student of Isaiah can also see His glory.

The tragedy of Israel's unbelief, in spite of all the evidence in Isaiah and elsewhere, is set forth in all its stark reality at the close of the book of Acts, and, as might be expected, it is set forth by a quotation from Isaiah.

The apostle Paul, following his customary procedure of giving the Jews an opportunity to accept Christ whenever he came to a new locality, spoke at length with the Jewish men of influence who would come to his home in Rome (where he was a prisoner in his own rented house). "From morning until evening" (Acts 28:23) he discussed with them the Old Testament Scriptures concerning Christ. The record states that he expounded the Law of Moses and the Prophets, and it is certain that Isaiah was referred to a great many times in the course of that momentous discussion. The results, from a human point of view, were disappointing:

And some were being persuaded by the things spoken, but others would not believe. And when they did not agree with one another, they began leaving after Paul had spoken one parting word, "The Holy Spirit rightly spoke through Isaiah the prophet to your fathers, saying,

'Go to this people and say,
"You will keep on hearing, but will not understand;
And you will keep on seeing, but will not perceive;
For the heart of this people has become dull,
And with their ears they scarcely hear,
And they have closed their eyes;
Lest they should see with their eyes,
And hear with their ears,
And understand with their heart and return,
And I should heal them."'

Let it be known to you therefore, that this salvation of God has been sent to the Gentiles; they will also listen." [Acts 28:24-28]

"The salvation of God" (or "the Lord") is the theme of this prophecy, of which the prophet's name (as will be shown) is the symbolic testimony. In accordance with the prophecy, the message has gone out to the Gentiles; the message of Christ is being proclaimed to "the ends of the earth."

THE NATURE OF PROPHECY

When people today speak of prophecy they customarily mean prediction of the future. But that is not the basic concept of prophecy in the Old Testament. The prophet was primarily a spokesman for God to the people of his generation—instructing, exhorting, and admonishing. Like the priest in Israel, he was an intermediary between God and men. But whereas the priest was man's representative to God—offering sacrifice and making intercession—the prophet was God's representative to men, delivering a message from God. Sometimes the same man held both offices, as in the case of Jeremiah (Jer. 1:1) and Ezekiel (Ezek. 1:3). It is unlikely that Isaiah was a priest as some have thought (because of his presence in the Temple when he had his great vision of God in Isaiah 6), for he says nothing about holding that office.

The New Testament declares that in former times God had spoken "to the fathers in the prophets in many portions and in many ways" (Heb. 1:1), and that prophecy did not originate with men, but "men moved by the Holy Spirit spoke from God" (2 Pet. 1:21). Isaiah was such a spokesman as described in those passages.

It would be a mistake, however, to exclude prediction from prophecy altogether. Though the prophet spoke to his own time, he also spoke to future times. Foretelling the future, it is clearly shown in Isaiah, is the prerogative of God alone (Isa. 46:9-10). The knowledge of the future that God revealed through the prophet was incontrovertible evidence that his entire message came from God and that he was not a mere preacher who launched out on his own.

The certainty of the future that God foretells is based not merely on the fact that God knows ahead of time what will take place, but on the fact that He is the sovereign Creator of history, just as He is the Creator of matter and of all things. The future is certain because it is within the all-compassing decree of the sovereign God (see Isa. 44:6—45:25).

Consequently, in Isaiah we can expect to find both the near view and the far view. God had messages that He gave through His servant to the kings and other people of Isaiah's time to meet the exigencies of life in their day, but He also gave words about coming events and even far distant prospects. The judgments of the turbulent Assyrian period in which Isaiah lived and ministered also foreshadowed greater judgments to come: the Babylonian captivity a century after Isaiah's lifetime; and the far distant judgments of the end time, that terrible "Day of the Lord" mentioned by a number of the prophets, still future after twenty-six centuries.

Those near and far views, however, are not restricted to judgment, for Isaiah is emphatically a prophet of consolation. He is permitted by God to see not only the return from the Babylonian captivity, to be brought about by the Persian king Cyrus in the sixth century B.C., but also the future millennial reign of the Messiah, a time of glorious righteousness and peace on this earth. No book of the Bible has more to say about that in more breathtaking language than Isaiah.

THE HISTORICAL BACKGROUND OF ISAIAH

The historical background of Isaiah is found in 2 Kings 15-20 and 2 Chronicles 26-32. Isaiah 37 and 2 Kings 19 are identical. Isaiah's ministry spanned the latter half of the eighth century before Christ.

For two hundred years the kingdom of Judah had been ruled by descendants of David, a lineage of both evil and good men. The divine assessment brands Ahaz as one who "did not do what was right in the sight of the LORD his God" (2 Kings 16:2); but the other three kings mentioned in Isaiah's prophecy were among the eight good kings of Judah (2 Kings 15:3, 34; 18:3). Even Uzziah (called Azariah in 2 Kings 15:1) is characterized in that way, in spite of his sin in later life of intruding into the priestly office contrary to the command of God. Scripture describes him as "so proud that he acted corruptly," and as "unfaithful to the LORD his God," explaining that he "entered the temple of the LORD to burn incense on the altar of incense" (2 Chron. 26:16). During the closing years of his life he bore the disease of leprosy in his body as God's judgment on his effrontery, and his son Jotham reigned in his stead.

Uzziah's long reign of fifty-two years was a time of domestic prosperity and greatness in foreign relations. It overlapped for some years with the lengthy reign of Jeroboam II of the house of Jehu in Israel, during which time the Northern Kingdom also was very prosperous. One great difficulty was that the outward prosperity caused many to forget God. The warning that God had given through Moses was disregarded and consequently took effect: "Then watch yourself, lest you forget the LORD" (Deut. 6:12; see the context in vv. 10-25). In both kingdoms the spiritual decline led to apostasy. Conditions in Israel were especially grave, as portrayed in Amos and Hosea, but Judah was not exempt, as Isaiah clearly shows.

The death of King Uzziah, which took place in the same year that Isaiah had his remarkable vision of the Lord (6:1), was probably in 740 B.C. That date gives a chronological reference point by which to date some of the other events in the book. The Assyrian invasion under Sennacherib, described in Isaiah 36, probably occurred in 701 B.C., although it must be admitted that there are chronological difficulties (see the commentary on chap.

36). Those two events give a span of approximately forty years, not quite enough to encompass the prophecies of the entire book.

Hezekiah's death probably came in 686 B.C. Although Hezekiah's son, Manasseh, is not mentioned in the superscription of Isaiah's prophecy, ancient tradition asserts that Isaiah's ministry continued into the early years of that wicked ruler's reign, and that the prophet was put to death by Manasseh, who allegedly used a most cruel and unusual form of execution by having the prophet sawn in two. Many believe that the reference to that terrible method of torture in Hebrews 11:37 alludes to Isaiah. That is possible but uncertain.

From the dates given in Isaiah it can be surmised that the prophecies are arranged in chronological order (see 6:1; 7:1; 14:28; 20:1; 36:1).

Although many nations are in view in Isaiah's prophecy and his vision extends to the whole world, the focus is on his own country of Judah and his own city, Jerusalem (1:1). He was aware of events in the Northern Kingdom (Israel) but dealt with them primarily as they affected Judah. The superscriptions of prophetical books of that period show that Amos and Hosea were somewhat older contemporaries. Amos, although from the town of Tekoa in Judah, prophesied primarily to Israel, as did Hosea (Amos 1:1; Hos. 1:1; 7:1).

The notation about the reigns at the beginning of Micah indicates that he, like Isaiah, was a prophet to Judah, beginning his ministry somewhat later than Isaiah.

PLACE OF ISAIAH IN THE CANON

The ancient Hebrews classified as prophetical books some that we consider historical, as well as those we call prophetical. The rationale for including a book among the prophets seems to have been that the writer held the *office* of prophet as well as possessing the prophetic *gift*.

That explains why Joshua, Judges, 1 and 2 Samuel, and 1 and 2 Kings were called the "Former Prophets." The five books of Moses, of course, stood in a class by themselves and were called the "Law" (Torah). The writers of the books of the Former Prophets were official spokesmen for God in their day, even though the contents of their books were historical, not prophetic in the restricted sense of prediction.

The "Latter Prophets" were Isaiah, Jeremiah, Ezekiel, and "The Twelve." The twelve are those books often called the Minor Prophets because of their relative brevity.

While it is true that Isaiah came chronologically before Jeremiah and Ezekiel, he did not come before every one of the twelve. Perhaps his book is placed at the head of that division of the Old Testament Scriptures because of its importance—its unprecedented portrayal of the coming Messiah, the one known in the New Testament as the Lord and Savior, Jesus Christ.

The Writer of the Book

The writer is Isaiah the son of Amoz. More is known about him than about most Old Testament prophets. Who Amoz was is not known, although there have been some conjectures linking him with the royal family of Judah. Obviously, he is not to be confused with the prophet Amos, who ministered to the kingdom of Israel slightly before Isaiah's time. The Hebrew names *Amos* and *Amoz* are quite distinct in spelling.

There is no proof of the validity of the ancient Hebrew tradition of Isaiah's relationship to the Davidic dynasty. He seems to have had considerable contact with the kings of his time, but that was more likely because he had to approach them as God's messenger rather than because of a family relationship.

It is known that Isaiah was married (see 8:3, where his wife is called "the prophetess"). The record clearly indicates that he lived in the city of Jerusalem. At the time of his commissioning he was in the Temple, but that does not necessarily mean that he was a priest, as has already been noted.

Isaiah had at least two sons, for two names are given: Shear-jashub (7:3) and Maher-shalal-hash-baz (8:3). The information is added that those two, as well as the prophet himself, were "for signs and wonders in Israel" (8:18); that is, they had symbolic names that indicated God's dealings not only with them but with the nation.

The Prophet's Name as the Theme

It is difficult on the surface to find a central theme in Isaiah from which all the material flows. Since there are two clearly defined parts, it almost appears that there should be two central themes, one for chapters 1-39 and another for chapters 40-66. It is obvious that part one speaks primarily of judgment, whereas part two emphasizes comfort. But are those mutually exclusive? Is there not a unifying thought that blends those two great themes together?

The problem can be stated as follows: What principle governs both judgment and comfort? A full answer can come only from a complete induction of the book. Careful study shows that the judgment is not unrelieved judgment, but that it is more than retribution for sin. It also includes restoration—blessing after the judgment. The term *restoration* describes the change in the whole structure of the cosmos, which is evident throughout the book. Reference is made repeatedly to the Lord's standard, which has been broken time and again not only by Israel but also by the other nations of the world. The sections dealing with the blessings of the kingdom show a restoration of the Lord's created order. He did not create the world "a waste" (45:18). The role of the Servant of the Lord will be to deliver justice or order to the world. The Lord promises Israel that it will be restored and smelted, and then Zion will be called a city of righteousness (1:24-26).

So the central or dominant theme of the whole book can be expressed as *the Lord's restoration of His created order*. That is the meaning of the expression so gloriously evident in the prophecy— the Lord's salvation through the Messiah (the Servant) "to the ends of the earth." (See appendix 1 for an inductive validation of the central theme.)

Actually, the prophet's name discloses the theme of his message. The name means "The salvation of the Lord," or "The Salvation of Yahweh."

The older, traditional spelling, *Jehovah*, is one of a series of accommodations to the ancient Hebrew reverential feeling, which amounted almost to superstition. The pious Israelite would not even pronounce that special name for God, considering it too sacred to be placed on his lips. It is regarded in the Old Testament as the special, personal, individual, covenant-making, and covenant-keeping name of the one true and living God and is made up of four letters (the *tetragrammaton,* naturally all consonants, for the Hebrew alphabet contains no vowels, and based on the root of the Hebrew verb "to be"). This name was explained by God to Moses at the burning bush (Ex. 3:14) and is paraphrased in the Greek New Testament as the One "who is and who was and who is to come" (Rev. 1:4).

The ancient Hebrews substituted the name *Adonai* (Lord) for the ineffable name, and that tradition was continued in the

Septuagint, the Greek translation of the Old Testament, where the word *Kurios* (Lord) is used. The Latin Vulgate (*Dominus*) and various English versions follow the same principle.

The vowel points of *Adonai* superimposed on the four consonants led to the traditional English pronunciation of *Jehovah*, a name that has become established in English hymnody. The *American Standard Version* (1901) attempted to popularize the form, but without success. Many modern scholars prefer the form "Yahweh," but because the word was not pronounced in ancient times, there is no way of knowing its exact pronunciation with certainty. Modern English translations for the most part have followed the traditional practice of substituting the word LORD to distinguish it from other words for "Lord"). The *New American Standard Bible*, the *New International Version*, the King James Version, and the *New King James Version* follow that practice.

The theme of Isaiah in broad, general terms is "The Lord's salvation to the ends of the earth" (49:6), reflecting the prophet's name. That salvation, prefigured in a sense by the deliverance from Babylon under Cyrus, is a worldwide deliverance through the Messiah, the One pictured so graphically in the book as the Servant of the Lord (Yahweh). Isaiah's vision is indeed worldwide, taking in a great multitude of Gentiles in addition to God's chosen people, Israel. That worldwide characteristic will appear often in the course of the investigation of this wonderful book.

The prophet Isaiah and King Hezekiah in the eighth century before Christ had a clearer idea of ethical monotheism than many people today. Careful observation of that truth in the book will help one avoid being deceived by the application of evolutionary ideas to the history of religion, a concept that has misled so many.

THE UNITY OF ISAIAH

The book of Isaiah is one of those portions of the Word of God often maligned and rejected. Its unity has been denied, its authorship questioned, and its authenticity impugned. For at least two hundred years unbelievers and destructive critics have tried to tear Isaiah to shreds.

It has long been considered fashionable and scholarly to refer to *Deutero-Isaiah* and, in a somewhat lesser degree, to *Trito-Isaiah*. Some scholars have tried to divide the book into many more than three documents, postulating a variety of writers and redactors, or critical editors, over a period of several centuries.

In the nineteenth century a great many interpreters believed that the eighth-century B.C. Isaiah wrote only chapters 1-39 (or less), and that the second part of the book (chaps. 40-66) was written by an unknown prophet (seer, or poet) in Babylon in the sixth century B.C., just before or at the time of the return from exile.

Later, it became commonplace to limit the Deutero-Isaiah to chapters 40-55 and to attribute the last chapters to a third author (Trito-Isaiah) in Palestine after the return from the captivity, perhaps in the fifth century B.C.

A number of helpful and scholarly works have been produced to prove the unity of Isaiah.[1] This study will touch on the subject only briefly, but the present authors are convinced that it is an essential matter. In the face of the evidence, and the relationship of this book to the rest of the Bible, a denial of the unity is tantamount to a rejection of its message.

A firm adherence to the unity of the book is demanded by a number of considerations in the areas of both external and internal evidence.

EXTERNAL EVIDENCE

1. *Uniform ancient Hebrew tradition.* First, there is the uniform testimony of the ancient Hebrew scholars who never doubted that Isaiah was one book by one author. Each of the books of the Latter Prophets begins with the author's name. Isaiah has only one name and only one beginning in all known manuscripts and versions. The magnificent Isaiah scroll discovered at Qumran and dated in the middle of the second century B.C., like all other manuscripts, is a unified book.

Add to that the testimony of the Septuagint and other ancient versions, and the witness of the Jewish historian Josephus in the first century A.D.

2. *Uniform Christian tradition.* To the uniform Hebrew tradition may be added the complete agreement of the writers of the early church; and not only the early writers, but

1. See especially Oswald T. Allis, *The Unity of Isaiah.*

apparently all such writers up until the eighteenth century. So far as can be determined, no one questioned the unity of Isaiah for approximately twenty-five-hundred years. In the latter half of the eighteenth century, men who were given over to humanism, naturalism, and skepticism began to question Isaiah's unity, along with destructive views about the authorship of the Pentateuch, the date of Daniel, the historicity of Jonah, and other similar attacks on the integrity and authority of the Word of God.

3. *Testimony of New Testament writers.* In addition to the external evidence of the uniform Hebrew and Christian traditions, an even more significant evidence is the consistent testimony of the New Testament writers, who quote from all parts of the book of Isaiah and attribute each quotation to the same author—Isaiah. Those quotations will be noted later.

4. *Testimony of the Lord Jesus Christ.* Above all the other lines of evidence is the personal testimony of the Lord Jesus Christ, who refers to different parts of Isaiah as originating from the same book. For example, when He read from the Scriptures in the synagogue at Nazareth, He turned to the book of the prophet Isaiah. But the portion He read (as recorded in Luke 4:18-19) was the beginning of Isaiah 61, which according to the critical theories could not have been written by Isaiah the son of Amoz. In fact, that part, according to the theory, was not even written by the Deutero-Isaiah, but by the Trito-Isaiah, or possibly even by some later redactor. The Lord Jesus Himself said it was Isaiah. That ought to be enough for any Christian.

INTERNAL EVIDENCE

The internal evidence of unity is very strong. In addition to the obvious unity in all the manuscripts of Isaiah, there is a uniform style throughout the book in spite of allegations to the contrary. That uniform style is observed most clearly in Isaiah's particularly apt use of distinctive leading ideas or motifs.

1. *The Holy One of Israel.* That expression is a characterization of the Lord and occurs twenty-five times in Isaiah. It

occurs only six times elsewhere in the Old Testament, including 2 Kings 19, a section identical to Isaiah 37. No doubt that title for God came from Isaiah's crucial experience described in Isaiah 6:1-13. The continual worship by the seraphim made such a deep impression on Isaiah that he forever after thought of the Lord as preeminently the "Holy One of Israel."[2]

The twenty-five occurrences of the title are divided between chapters 1-39 (12 times) and chapters 40-66 (13 times), the supposed Deutero-Isaiah.

2. *The mouth of the Lord has spoken.* Here is an expression that is found only in Isaiah (1:20; 40:5; and 58:14). Those three places come respectively from what the critics call Isaiah, Deutero-Isaiah, and Trito-Isaiah. Can that be accidental? Along with the other cumulative evidences, is it not conceivable that the divine author, the Holy Spirit of God, prompted Isaiah to include that assertion in the three places where it was needed to support the unity of the book?

3. *Other examples of the "circle of ideas."* There are other repeated expressions in addition to these which George L. Robinson calls the "circle of ideas."[3] One such is the mention of the "highway" (see 11:16; 35:8; 40:3; 43:19; 49:11; 57:14; 62:10). Another is the repeated reference to the "remnant" (see 1:9, KJV; 10:20-22; 11:11, 16; 14:22, 30, KJV; 15:9; 16:14; 17:3; 21:17; 28:5; 37:31; 46:3; cf. 65:8-9).

Still another example of Isaiah's literary style is his use of "emphatic reduplication" (see 2:7-8; 6:3; 8:9; 24:16, 23; 40:1; 43:11, 25; 48:15; 51:12; 57:19; 62:10).

In summing up arguments from literary style Robinson comments, "In fact, it is not extravagant to say that Isaiah's style differs widely from that of every other Old Testament prophet, and is as far removed as possible from that of Ezekiel and the post-exilic prophets."[4]

---

2. Occurrences of the title are found in 1:4; 5:19; 5:24; 10:20; 12:6; 17:7; 29:19; 30:11; 30:12; 30:15; 31:1; 37:23; 41:14; 41:16; 41:20; 43:3; 43:14; 45:11; 47:4; 48:17; 49:7; 54:5; 55:5; 60:9; 60:14.
3. George L. Robinson, "Isaiah," in *The International Standard Bible Encyclopedia*, 3:1505.
4. Ibid., 3:1506.

4. *The messianic content as a unifying factor.* The constant references to the Messiah, particularly as the "Servant of the Lord," bind the book together into a unity. The messianic character of Isaiah is well known, but even to one who is familiar with the book there are always new and almost startling evidences of the presence of the Lord Jesus Christ.

A life of Christ could almost be written from the allusions in Isaiah. This book is the locus of the prophecy of the virgin birth (7:14). It tells of the Messiah in His humility as a "root out of parched ground" (53:2), but also in His royal heritage, as the "shoot . . . from the stem of Jesse" (11:1), as the "costly cornerstone" (28:16), as the "king [who] will reign righteously" (32:1), as God's "chosen one in whom [He] delights" (42:1), as the suffering Servant on whom the Lord laid "the iniquity of us all" (53:6), but the resurrected One who "will prolong His days" (53:10), and as the Proclaimer of "the favorable year of the LORD" (61:2) and "the day of vengeance of our God" (v. 2), as He comes in judgment and treads "the wine trough alone" (63:3).

The Lord Jesus' use of Isaiah 61 in the synagogue at Nazareth is instructive. He read only a portion of the particular prophecy (Luke 4:18-19; Isa. 61:1-2*a*) and announced, "Today this Scripture has been fulfilled in your hearing" (Luke 4:21). That is an illustration of the intertwining of the two advents of Christ in one prophecy, a reality of which Peter informed us (1 Pet. 1:10-12). In several other places we observe the same phenomenon.

5. *The argument of chapters 40-48.* These chapters center on the deliverance from Babylon. This portion, which will be discussed in some detail later, mentions Cyrus by name, compares the all-powerful God with the powerless idols of the nations, and views the deliverance from Babylon as foreshadowing a greater deliverance through the Messiah, when He will change the entire world. The Lord's Servant is on a mission of salvation to the Gentiles during which He will effect justice and restore order to the earth. The Lord promises to regather His unworthy servant Israel to the land, using a Gentile power to do that and to restore Temple worship. He promises that the Gentile world will

bow down eventually to a redeemed Israel, for Israel is His chosen people.

The argument of these chapters, especially that of chapter 43, depends on authorship before the Babylonian captivity or all integrity is lost. Furthermore, the description of the land is obviously written by someone living in it, not someone living in Babylon.

BACKGROUND OF THE CRITICAL VIEWS OF ISAIAH

One of the major starting points of the doubts about the unity and integrity of the book of Isaiah seems to have been the plain and direct mention of Cyrus in chapters 44 and 45. Of course, anyone who did not know God would find it hard to believe that a prophet writing in the eighth century before Christ could know about the Persian king Cyrus, who lived in the sixth century before Christ, some two hundred years later.

If Isaiah were merely a human book, one might well understand the questions and even the denials of the investigators. But it is not merely a human book. It is part of Holy Scripture, and Isaiah was one of those men who "spoke from God" as they were "moved by the Holy Spirit" (2 Pet. 1:21). This line of thought will be pursued in later sections of the commentary.

THE USE OF ISAIAH IN THE NEW TESTAMENT

There are numerous places in the New Testament where Isaiah is quoted or alluded to. In fact, Isaiah is referred to in the New Testament more often than any other Old Testament book except the Psalms.

Matthew uses Isaiah to show that Jesus of Nazareth is the promised Messiah and King (Matt. 4:14; 8:17; 12:17). When John the Baptizer began his ministry as the forerunner of the Lord Jesus he quoted Isaiah, showing himself to be the fulfiller of the prophecy of the voice crying in the wilderness (John 1:23). As previously noted, the Lord Jesus Himself read from Isaiah in the synagogue at Nazareth (Luke 4:18-19).

The apostle John reports that Isaiah, in his vision of God, spoke of the glory of the Lord Jesus (John 12:41).

The Ethiopian treasurer, returning home after worshiping in Jerusalem, was reading Isaiah when the Holy Spirit directed Philip to join him and instruct him (Acts 8:28).

Paul, in both his sermons and discourses and in his writings, quotes Isaiah (Acts 28:25-27; Rom. 9:27, 29; 10:16, 20; 15:12).

References to Isaiah in the New Testament are not limited to those passages in which the prophet's name is used. Sometimes he is quoted simply as one of the prophets. (See Appendix 2 for quotations of Isaiah in the New Testament.)

FURTHER THOUGHTS ON ISAIAH'S STYLE

Mention was made earlier of the unifying theme of Isaiah that weaves together the two main parts of the book. Isaiah has been compared to a great symphony in which two dominant themes and many lesser themes are harmonized. The two major themes are judgment and comfort, announced respectively in chapters 1 and 40. As previously noted, Isaiah looks toward the Babylonian captivity and beyond that to the return—deliverance through Cyrus. But the deliverance goes far beyond that deliverance from exile—there is salvation from sin and from death through Immanuel, the Messiah, to Israel and the Gentiles; and that salvation extends to the "ends of the earth" (52:10).

The two themes keep recurring in new and interesting forms and variations, but the order is never reversed: judgment is followed by comfort.

The style of Isaiah is rich and varied. His vocabulary is very extensive. Figures of speech abound, for the language is frequently poetic, even though Isaiah is not classified among the poetical books. The poetic form can be seen by observing the printed pages in the *New American Standard Bible*, the *New International Version*, or the *New King James Version*.

Although one could not strictly speak of the whole book as one magnificent song, it does contain a number of recognizable songs, such as the song of the vineyard (chap. 5), the song of the coming salvation (chap. 12), the song of the rejoicing desert (chap. 35), the song of the restored wife (chap. 54), and others. Even some of the prophecies of judgment, the "woes" and the "burdens," are poetic dirges, lamenting the sin that must bring retribution from God.

Personification, metaphor, simile, and other figures of speech are numerous in the book. There are instances of paronomasia, or play on words, which are not usually evident in translation. Such examples are found in the song of the vineyard in chapter 5:

> Thus He looked for justice [*mishpat*], but behold, bloodshed [*mispah*]; for righteousness [*sedaqah*], but behold, a cry of distress [*seaqah*]. [5:7]

Alliteration (which, like paronomasia, does not lend itself well to translation) is also prominent. The use of a refrain is a frequent literary device that can be carried over into translation.

Another characteristic of Isaiah's style is his use of satire. Where can one find a more scathing denunciation of idolatry—so prevalent even among the people of Judah—than in Isaiah's mocking comment about the man who cuts down a tree, uses part of it to make a fire to warm himself and to cook his food, and then makes another part of it into a "god" (44:13-20)?

BASIC OUTLINE OF THE BOOK

As indicated before, the simplest and most logical outline of Isaiah is that which recognizes two main parts. The difference between those parts is considered by some to be so marked that they are conceived of as being two distinct literary productions. Those who hold that view tend to overstress the differences and minimize the similarities and recurring themes, and to overlook the essential harmony of the two parts into one grand theme of redemption.

At any rate, there is a recognizable change of tone at the beginning of chapter 40. It requires no great knowledge of the book to label the first part "Judgment" and the second part "Comfort." In each case the dominant note is struck at the very beginning: God's severe but just indictment of Judah in chapter 1, and God's call to speak comforting words to Jerusalem after her long trials in chapter 40. Hence, the basic outline is apparent even to the casual reader:

JUDGMENT FROM GOD (1:1—39:8)
COMFORT FROM GOD (40:1—66:24)

In seeking to analyze those main parts, one needs to discover subdivisions in the book itself and not foist them onto the book. It is impossible at this late date to devise a completely original outline (indeed, if it were original, it probably would be untrue or at least inaccurate). What should be done is to recognize the divisions that are intrinsic to the text itself.

Almost all commentators seem to see a unity and continuity in the first six chapters leading up to the call of the prophet of God after his encounter with the "Holy One of Israel," as described in chapter 6.

Similarly, the prophecies in the troubled times of Ahaz (chaps. 7-12), when Assyria was threatening with such menace, are seen to center around the One called Immanuel. In fact, some of the interpreters call those chapters "The Book of Immanuel."

Chapters 13-23 form a distinct division, with the unifying word being *burden* (KJV*). The *New American Standard Bible* uses the word *oracle*, but indicates in a note that the Hebrew text is literally "burden." The meaning is that those prophecies are heavy or grievous in the sense of predicting doom. They tell of unrelieved judgment on various Gentile nations.

Chapters 24-27, sometimes called "Isaiah's little apocalypse," form a unity as they describe events of the end time, the familiar order of judgment followed by comfort.

The unifying term in chapters 28-33 is the word *woe*, again introducing God's certain judgment for sin.

Two chapters follow with a repetition of the theme, setting forth God's indignation followed by the glory of the future, pictured by the desert blossoming like a rose (chaps. 34-35).

Chapters 36-39 are usually called a "historical interlude." Some prefer to call this a separate division and to view the book in three main parts:

JUDGMENT (1:1—35:10)
HISTORICAL (36:1—39:8)
COMFORT (40:1—66:24)

However, it seems more convenient and more accurate to view chapters 36-39 as a part of the total picture of judgment. They give the outcome of the Assyrian invasion of Judah (thus connecting with the first part) and provide the explanation of the coming Babylonian captivity so much in view, either directly or indirectly, throughout the book. In whatever way one takes this historical interlude, it furnishes the logical bridge from the prophet's day to the exile in the next century. That in Isaiah's day Babylon was not

---

* King James Version.

a world power that could counter the might of Assyria adds to the amazing nature of Isaiah's prophecy. Babylon became such a power very rapidly in the century between Isaiah's and Jeremiah's times.

OUTLINE OF THE FIRST PART OF ISAIAH
The Judgment of God (1:1—39:8)

I. Opening Prophecies: God's Case Against Sinful Judah (1:1—6:13)
II. Prophecies Centering on Immanuel (7:1—12:6)
III. Oracles (Burdens) Against the Nations (13:1—23:18)
IV. Punishment Followed by Kingdom Blessing (24:1—27:13)
V. The Woes (28:1—33:24)
VI. Indignation and Glory (34:1—35:10)
VII. Historical Interlude (36:1—39:8)

ANALYSIS OF THE SECOND PART OF ISAIAH

In the second part of the book the Holy Spirit shows Isaiah the return from the Babylonian exile and uses that return as a foreshadowing of the greater deliverance to come through the Messiah. From that ideal point of view Isaiah can see the captivity as past (although it did not begin until about a century after his lifetime) and can rejoice in the glories of Israel's restoration.

The German commentator Rückert in 1831 was evidently one of the earliest to observe that the second part of Isaiah is made up of twenty-seven brief sections corresponding roughly to the chapter divisions as they now exist.[5] They are clearly grouped into three sections of nine chapters each. That threefold division is embedded in the book by the use of the refrain "There is no peace for the wicked" (48:22; 57:21).

It seems most unlikely that the symmetrical arrangement of the second part of Isaiah could be accidental or coincidental. The inner structure of each of the three sections is intricate and calls for more detailed investigation (in connection with those chapters in the commentary).

The section containing chapters 40-48 tells of the coming deliverance from Babylon through the Persian ruler Cyrus, who is named in chapters 44 and 45. As God's "anointed" (the only

5. *Translation of the Hebrew Prophets*, cited by Franz Delitzsch, *Biblical Commentary on the Prophecies of Isaiah*, 2:128.

Gentile ruler so designated in Scripture) he becomes a type, or prophetic symbol, of "the anointed one" (Hebrew, *Messiah*; Greek, *Christ*) through whom greater deliverance comes. In this section God draws a contrast between Himself and the false "gods" of the pagan nations.

Chapters 49-57, forming the central section of the second part, have as their main theme the two great lines of messianic prophecy mentioned in the New Testament: "the sufferings of Christ and the glories to follow" (1 Pet. 1:11). The central thought is on the suffering Servant of the Lord as the Redeemer.

The last section, chapters 58-66, climaxes the teaching of God's purpose for Israel and describes the coming glory for that chosen nation.

OUTLINE OF THE SECOND PART OF ISAIAH

Part Two: The Comfort of God (40:1—66:24)
I. Deliverance of God's People (40:1—48:22)
II. The Suffering Servant as the Redeemer (49:1—57:21)
III. The Glorious Consummation (58:1—66:24)

1

Opening Prophecies: The Lord's Case Against Judah

(1:1 — 6:13)

The unity of chapters 1 through 6 is reinforced by the description of Isaiah's unusual experience of seeing the Lord (6:1-13) and by the additional time note in 7:1 that obviously begins a new section.

Judah's persistent and continuous hardening of heart is seen in these opening prophecies. It is first made evident by God's indictment in 1:2-23 and is further portrayed in the song of the Lord's vineyard in 5:1-30. In between those two statements assurance is given of future kingdom blessings in spite of the judgments that must inevitably come. Thus, even at the beginning, the eventual purpose of God in restoring His created order is realized.

The section can be outlined as follows:

PART ONE: THE JUDGMENT OF GOD (1:1—39:8)

I. Opening Prophecies (1:1—6:13)
  A. God's Lament over Judah's Corruption (1:1-31)
    1. Heading of the whole book (1:1)
    2. God's indictment (1:2-23)
    3. God's vengeance (1:24-31)
  B. The Future Kingdom and Its Introductory Judgments (2:1—4:6)
    1. Messiah's reign (2:1-4)
    2. Appeal and warning (2:5—3:26)
    3. The Branch of the Lord (4:1-6)

C. Judah's Sins and the Resultant Woes (5:1-30)
   1. The song of the vineyard (5:1-6)
   2. The meaning of the song (5:7-30)
D. Isaiah's Call and Commission (6:1-13)
   1. The vision (6:1-4)
   2. Confession and cleansing (6:5-7)
   3. The prophet's commission (6:8-13)

HEADING OF THE WHOLE BOOK (1:1)

As is found in all the "Latter Prophets," Isaiah gives his name at the beginning of his book. Having an oral ministry of almost half a century, he undoubtedly was called on to speak much more for God than what is recorded. But this is the portion of his ministry that God was pleased to preserve for time and eternity in His inspired, inerrant Word.

In this case the name of the book is especially significant for at least two reasons:

1. *The attacks on the unity and the authorship of the entire book.* There is only one heading and only one name attached to the whole document. That has already been alluded to in the introduction where major arguments for the unity and genuineness of the whole book of Isaiah have been considered.

   There is no evidence of the book's ever having existed in any other form. The magnificent Isaiah scroll dated probably in the late second century B.C. is an ancient witness, as are the Septuagint and other pre-Christian translations. So also are the writings of the first-century Jewish historian, Josephus, who stated that Cyrus read about himself in the book of Isaiah.[1]

2. *The use made of the prophet's name in indicating the theme of the book.* That will become increasingly apparent in the course of the commentary.

The fact that Isaiah's message is called a *vision*, with the further explanation that *he saw* it, informs us that the prophet was the

---

1. Josephus (Flavius), *Antiquities of the Jews*, Book XI, chapter I, paragraph 2.

instrument or channel, not the originator of the message. God showed it to him by supernatural perception, as He did to the other writers of Scripture. Much prophecy is apocalyptic in nature; that is, it is revealed by God to and through the prophet in pictorial form. God also gives the prophet supernaturally the words in which to set it down as a part of the Word of God. That is not a mechanical dictation; instead, God works through the personality of the human writer without doing violence to it. Compare Paul in 1 Corinthians 2:10-11 and 2 Timothy 3:16-17, Peter in 2 Peter 1:20-21, and the writer to the Hebrews in Hebrews 1:1.

The message primarily concerns *Judah*, the Southern Kingdom, and its capital city, *Jerusalem*. The judgment of God is even more definitely emphasized when one realizes that Judah had advantages that other nations and even Israel (the Northern Kingdom) did not have. Through its entire history Judah was ruled by descendants of David, with whom God had made a special covenant (2 Sam. 7). Furthermore, the Temple worship was located in Jerusalem, which accents the awfulness of the apostasy. God's indictment is detailed and precise. It shows both the actual and the potential evil of the nation. Since Isaiah was looking toward the Babylonian captivity, which came a century after his own time, he was permitted to see not only how corrupt his own country was in his day, but also the depth of the degradation as it developed in the intervening time before the exile.

It was customary in Old Testament times to date documents by the reigns of various kings. The four mentioned here included three who were assessed as good (referred to in the introduction) and Ahaz, who was outstandingly wicked. The heading of Hosea (Hos. 1:1) shows that prophet to have been a contemporary of Isaiah, and the heading of Micah (Mic. 1:1) shows his ministry to have begun somewhat later than Isaiah. Amos evidently had brought his ministry to a close shortly before Isaiah began his (Amos 1:1).

In spite of the reforms under the godly King Hezekiah and similar reforms a century later under King Josiah (2 Kings 22:1—23:30), the kingdom of Judah was plunging headlong toward ruin, arrested somewhat in the two periods just mentioned. But as previously noted, it was going on inexorably toward its inevitable conclusion.

GOD'S INDICTMENT (1:2-23)

After the heading, God's indictment of Judah follows in solemn poetic language. It is viewed by many as an example of the lawsuit formula—a lawsuit against the nation for breaking the covenant.

The Hebrew term meaning *lawsuit* is not uncommon in the Scriptures. The root meaning of the word is "to strive" or "to contend." Because no courtroom can contain God, the whole created world is called upon to witness God's faithfulness to His people and the people's faithlessness to Him.

The call to heaven and earth to listen is reminiscent of Moses' prophetic song in Deuteronomy 32, where there is a like appeal to heaven and earth. The Lord is thus showing publicly His case against the sinful and rebellious kingdom.

"Sons I have reared and brought up" (v. 2). The relationship is expressed emphatically and affords a stark contrast with the conduct of the ox and the donkey, which are notorious for their stubbornness and stupidity. In spite of all the blessings that God had heaped on those people in a special relationship to Himself, they were persistently disobeying and rebelling. The Old Testament is very sparing in the use of the term *sons* in describing people's relationship to God, but here it is stressed to show the special quality of God's bounty on the people of Israel.

Note the use of the term *Israel* in verse 3. Although Isaiah was living in Judah and his message was addressed primarily to that kingdom, God is extending His judgment and His blessings to the totality of His chosen nation, because someday the breach will be healed and the division will be over forever.

"My people do not understand" (v. 3). In human relations no one likes to be misunderstood. Certainly God should have been understood by the people for whom He had done so much.

The parallelism of the Hebrew poetry is very apparent even in translation. The "sinful nation" (v. 4) is described in three further ways that emphasize the corruptness of both their nature and their deeds (original and personal sin). Instead of going forward with their gracious God, they turned backward from Him.

The tone of the Lord's words in this passage is not censorious, but sorrowful and pleading. God is not pleased with the sinfulness of His people nor with the punishment that His justice requires. It is important to see in this opening accusation the first occurrence of the name "the Holy One of Israel" (v. 4). A holy God must condemn sin. Isaiah had come face to face with God's holiness; hence, he was able to present God's case to the sinful people who were ignoring the truth.

"Why will you be stricken again?" the Lord asks (v. 5), since the whole "body politic" is presented as being completely covered with wounds and bruises. "Why" (KJV) seems more accurate and appropriate than "Where" (NASB*). The condition described in these verses is a beginning of the fulfillment of the curses pronounced on Israel for disobedience, as recorded in Leviticus 26 and Deuteronomy 28.

Although some of the commentators have regarded that as a description of a person in an advanced stage of leprosy, it seems more likely to refer to a body that has been covered with wounds from hard blows.

Verse 7 and following are taken by some as alluding to Isaiah's time, but it seems much more probable that the prophet is allowed by God to look ahead to the end result of the moral and spiritual corruption that was already so apparent in his day. The judgment is viewed as if it had already come and the vineyard is seen as stripped bare with only "a very small remnant" (v. 9, KJV) surviving. The doctrine of the remnant is prominent in Isaiah. God is not bringing complete destruction on the nation as He did on Sodom and Gomorrah (Gen. 19:1-29), although its sins were enough to warrant it.

One is startled to hear the nation actually addressed as Sodom and Gomorrah (v. 10). Many in Judah undoubtedly protested that they did not deserve to be compared to those wicked cities. An added evil of their corruption was that they were going through the forms of religious worship. They kept the outward requirements of the Mosaic ritual that God Himself had given. But God called their sacrifices "worthless offerings" (v. 13). They were only trampling God's courts, in effect wearing out the Temple pavement for no purpose whatever except outward, hypocritical show.

* *New American Standard Bible.*

The hands that they held out in supplication to God were stained with bloodshed (v. 15). They were oppressors and murderers.

God is always gracious, merciful, and longsuffering. He called on the people (v. 16) to cleanse themselves and to substitute righteousness for unrighteousness, but then in His grace He provided the cleansing they needed:

> "Come now, and let us reason together,"
> Says the LORD,
> "Though your sins are as scarlet,
> They will be as white as snow;
> Though they are red like crimson,
> They will be like wool."

[verse 18]

The general teaching of the Bible is clear that cleansing from sin is based on the substitutionary sacrifice of the Lord Jesus Christ, the sacrifice that is portrayed so graphically elsewhere in Isaiah (see esp. chap. 53). Israel could give no defense, but God extended grace to her. However, when grace is refused there is nothing left but judgment (v. 20). In this verse is the first of the three occurrences of the expression "The mouth of the Lord has spoken" (see also 40:5 and 58:14).

The covenant relationship of God with His people is viewed a number of times in the Old Testament as analogous to the marriage relationship. In this section the city that once had been faithful to God is viewed as most unfaithful: "The faithful city has become a harlot" (v. 21). The corruption of Judah is pictured in practical ways, emphasizing justice in day-to-day relationships. The rulers are especially blamed because of their greater privileges and general influence on the people.

GOD'S VENGEANCE (1:24-31)

When God announced His vengeance on the wicked rulers and nation, He used a combination of names for Himself not found elsewhere in the book. First He called Himself *Adonai* (Lord), which has the idea of *sovereign Master*. In connection with that He used His special covenant name, Yahweh, and combined it with His control over the "hosts" or "armies" of heaven. Finally, as if that were not enough to emphasize His majesty and power, He called Himself the "Mighty One of Israel," the One who is able to do His will in spite of all opposition and rebellion. The names in combination assert God's omnipotence and show the absolute certainty of the judgment He will bring to pass.

The purpose of the judgment is not utter destruction, but eventual restoration (v. 26). God is faithful and has not forgotten His covenants with Abraham and David. The conditions of the Palestinian Covenant must be fulfilled as well, however, before the blessings of the other covenants can be realized.

The term *Zion* (v. 27) is used many times in Isaiah as a name for Jerusalem in its redeemed state, the dwelling place of God among His people.

MESSIAH'S REIGN (2:1-4)

Having seen the word of God concerning judgment on Judah and Jerusalem, the prophet is then permitted to see a word that relieves the judgment. It is as though God is seeking to reassure His people that out of the judgment—which is necessary and inevitable—must and will come future blessing and glory. A knowledge of what the future holds in blessing will enable God's people to undergo the trials of the intervening time.

The expression *the last days* (v. 2) in Isaiah refers to messianic times. Here the prophecy leaps across the ages from Isaiah's day to the future kingdom age. Many interpreters who have sought to identify Israel with the church explain those outstanding promises to Israel about a future kingdom on the earth as not to be fulfilled literally, but to be fulfilled spiritually—or rather, now being fulfilled spiritually—in the church. The number and content of such passages preclude any denial of their literalness. And, of course, in literal interpretation there is room for figurative language.

Isaiah obviously did not know the time of that coming kingdom. It could have been near or distant. He knew nothing about the church age because it had not been revealed in his day. The kingdom could have come in his day, but only after a return from exile as is revealed in chapters 40-48.

In Scripture, a mountain is sometimes used to represent a kingdom. When the mountain of the Lord's house is established at the top of the mountains, it will be a time when Israel is exalted among the nations with those from all nations looking to Israel for guidance.

That represents a decided change from the prophet's day and from any day between his time and the present. For a long time Israel has been despised by many of the great ones of this world. In fulfillment of the prophetic words given through Moses, Israel is considered by many to be the "tail" and not the "head" (Deut. 28:13). In the day described here the situation will be completely reversed.

A crucial question in determining anyone's eschatological position (his view of prophetic truth) is whether Israel as a nation has any future in God's plan. Isaiah contains a number of passages in which one either must acknowledge a future glory for Israel or retreat into allegory or "spiritualizing."

Here the prophet is allowed to look far ahead so that he and those whom he is addressing may not be overwhelmed by the weight of guilt on their people and the consequent judgment of God. Judgment must come and as noted previously, the first main part of Isaiah has judgment as its prominent theme. But it is as though God would make the judgment less unbearable by reminding that there is glory beyond the judgment. God's purpose for Israel will be fulfilled in the glorious earthly rule of the Messiah.

This passage is almost identical to the opening verses of Micah 4 (contrast Joel 3:10). It is useless to speculate which prophet made use of whose material. The most likely answer is that the Holy Spirit gave the same revelation to both.

This is a beautiful poetic (but none the less real and literal) description of the coming earthly kingdom of the Lord Jesus Christ. It should be compared not only with the parallel passage in Micah 4, but also with other kingdom passages such as Psalms 2 and 46.

There have always been yearnings for peace among nations. Almost all nations have professed to be "peaceloving." But there have always been the aggressor nations, such as Assyria in Isaiah's time and Babylon in Jeremiah's time.

The universal disarmament described here will come about not by the goodwill of nations or blocs of nations, but by the absolute domination of the Lord Jesus Christ, who singlehandedly will bring about peace on earth (cf. Isa. 9:6-7). With the Savior reigning, there can be disarmament because He will enforce righteousness on the earth. Men have talked about "benevolent despots," but no one has actually seen one. There will be One in the future day described here. (Note the word *despotes* used of Christ in 2 Peter 2:1.)

A further word needs to be added concerning the language of this prophecy. Some consider it a dilemma to talk about literal fulfillment in conjunction with the mention of ancient weapons no longer used in warfare, for example. Is it necessary to be speaking of literal swords and literal spears in order to have a literal fulfillment? The answer seems to be that the prophet must speak to his own time in language that his contemporaries can understand and yet speak to all times. Swords and spears are clearly understood in the passage as implements of warfare, just as plowshares and pruning hooks are tools of agriculture. All kinds of munitions and armaments will be converted to peaceful uses and processes. Military schools will then become unnecessary— "never again will they learn war" (v.4).

Many passages in the Old Testament speak of that future kingdom age. To seek a "spiritual" explanation, as though the Holy Spirit were somehow speaking of the blessings of the church now, is to lose touch with reality. This commentary will touch on other places in Isaiah where that future kingdom is prominent.

One would not deny that Christ gives peace *now* to the believing sinner, but one must not confuse peace on earth with what the Scripture calls "peace with God" (Rom. 5:1) or "the peace of God" (Phil. 4:7). There is no real peace of any kind apart from the Lord Jesus Christ.

APPEAL AND WARNING (2:5—3:26)

It is clear that the kingdom cannot be set up before a time of judgment. Consequently, the appeal and warning in this passage are extremely relevant. We see here a mingling of conditions in the prophet's day with conditions of a future day of judgment, the Day of the Lord—called here a "day of reckoning" (v. 12). The expression the *Day of the Lord*, found often in the prophets, including Isaiah, is distinguished from the present time, which is "man's day" (the literal meaning of 1 Cor. 4:3). God's dealings with the earth are being carried on indirectly now through His providence. In a future time He will intervene directly in judgment as He has done at times in the past, notably in the Noahic flood. This future intervention, described in many Old Testament prophetical passages and in the New Testament book of Revelation, will be on a worldwide scale (as the flood was) and will introduce the future kingdom age when the Lord Jesus Christ, returning personally, will rule over the earth. "He makes wars to cease to the end of the earth" (Ps. 46:9).

God's "day of reckoning" is against those who are "proud and lofty" (v. 12). Scripture has repeated statements about God's hatred of pride (see Prov. 3:34; James 4:6; 1 Pet. 5:5). His future judgment will bring down everything that is lifted up falsely.

This passage contains repetition of ideas, which is the genius of Hebrew poetry, and makes use of a refrain, characteristic of Isaiah (note vv. 7-8).

Some of the calamities mentioned in the passage obviously took place at the time of the Babylonian invasions and captivity, but much of the prophecy looks forward to "that day," a clear allusion to messianic times (v. 17). Idolatry, which figures so prominently in this book as the object of the prophet's satire, will ultimately be abolished (v. 18). Men's hiding themselves from "the terror of the LORD and the splendor of His majesty" (v. 21) is an end-time event, also mentioned in Revelation 6:15-17.

In His warning to the sinful nation God explains how He is going to remove the rulers and leaders and that He "will make mere lads their princes" (3:4). There is no doubt allusion to the troubled period of invasions. After the death of King Josiah from his wound at the battle of Megiddo, his descendants were mere puppets— Jehoahaz, of the king of Egypt; Jehoiakim, Jehoiachin, and Zedekiah, of the king of Babylon. They were all lacking in ability to govern. The underlying strain is that the people have brought the judgment on themselves through their sinfulness and rebellion (vv. 8-9). The leaders, as should be expected, have the strongest guilt (vv. 14-15), for they have abused their privileges and used their positions to their own advantage.

The women are not to escape the judgment of God any more than the men. The description of the luxurious fashions emphasizes the futility of trusting in outward adornment (note the contrast in 1 Pet. 3:3-4).

The closing verses of chapter 3 speak of the tremendous depletion of the male population through warfare. The first verse of chapter 4 actually belongs with chapter 3. The women will be willing to give up their rights that they could claim under the Mosaic law in order to have husbands (Ex. 21:10). The reference to "that day" (Isa. 4:1) must refer to the end of the tribulation period, because the same expression is used in 4:2 for the beginning of the kingdom.

THE BRANCH OF THE LORD (4:1-6)

The "Branch of the LORD" mentioned in verse 2 can be no other than the Messiah (cf. Jer. 23:5; 33:15; Zech. 3:8; 6:12). The mark of distinction in "that day" will not be position or prestige, but holiness (v. 3). In beautiful poetic language the Lord shows how His presence will abide with His people (v. 5) as it did in earlier times during their wilderness journeys. God will be a shelter both from the burning sun and the destructive rainstorms (v. 6).

It is remarkable how many times in Isaiah the same sequence of events is covered; events connected with the future judgment of Israel and the kingdom age when the Lord Jesus Christ will reign over the earth.

THE SONG OF THE VINEYARD (5:1-30)

God now announces judgment in the form of a poetic parable. Its presentation as a "song" (v. 1) may serve to soften the severity of the prophecy. It shows the favored position that Israel enjoyed. The interpretation is clear because it is given in the passage itself (v. 7). There are other places in the Old Testament in which Israel is called a vine or a vineyard (cf. Ps. 80:8 and Hos. 10:1).

The parable of the vineyard given by the Lord Jesus Christ (Matt. 21:33-44) undoubtedly was designed as a parallel to this passage. The Pharisees and chief priests clearly perceived that the Lord directed His parable against them.

Since God Himself had planted the vineyard, He had a right to expect good results from it. Instead of justice, however, He found oppression; instead of righteousness, He found the cry of the oppressed (v. 7).

Some of the sins of Israel that bring this judgment are plainly enumerated. Grasping greediness will be punished by barren fields, indicative of extensive crop failure (vv. 8-10). Drunkenness will be punished with captivity (vv. 11-14). God will see to it that men will be brought down and that He Himself will be exalted (vv.15-17).

Woe is pronounced against those who are defiant and rebellious (vv. 18-19) and against those who confuse moral issues, failing to differentiate between right and wrong (v. 20)—a sin that is fully as prevalent today as in Isaiah's day.

Further, woe is pronounced against those who in their conceit depend on their own faulty human wisdom (v. 21), and against the drunken judges (vv. 22-23). The incidence of alcoholism in governmental circles in the twentieth century is terrifying, and is as widespread as it was in Judah when God announced that He would not excuse and would not spare.

In view of the apostate condition of Israel, God must surely intervene in judgment. His justice is invoked first in a general statement of their despising "the word of the Holy One of Israel" (v. 24). Next it is pictured as a blow from His hand (v. 25); finally it is seen as an invading army (vv. 26-30).

Having faithfully conveyed God's indictment to the sinful nation, the prophet completes the first section of the book by narrating his call from God to the prophetic office.

ISAIAH'S CALL AND COMMISSION (6:1-13)

Everywhere one looks in Isaiah one can find some intimation of the Messiah as the promised Redeemer and eventual King of Israel and the earth. In discerning Him, however, the careful student must not indulge his imagination, but must stand on the firm ground of Scripture's teaching.

The connection of Isaiah 6 with the Lord Jesus Christ is clearly stipulated in the New Testament. That could be known even apart from explicit statement, because the Lord Jesus was directly involved in every theophany, or appearance of God, in the Old Testament (see John 1:18). But there is explicit statement.

In accounting for the hardness of heart and the rejection of Christ by the religious leaders of His day, the apostle John quotes from two passages in Isaiah:

> But though He had performed so many signs before them, yet they were not believing in Him; that the word of Isaiah the prophet might be fulfilled, which he spoke, "LORD, WHO HAS BELIEVED OUR REPORT? AND

TO WHOM HAS THE ARM OF THE LORD BEEN REVEALED?" [Isa. 53:1] For this cause they could not believe, for Isaiah said again, "HE HAS BLINDED THEIR EYES, AND HE HARDENED THEIR HEART; LEST THEY SEE WITH THEIR EYES, AND PERCEIVE WITH THEIR HEART, AND BE CONVERTED, AND I HEAL THEM." [Isa. 6:10] These things Isaiah said, because he saw His glory, and he spoke of Him. [John 12:37-41]

"His glory" in this context can only mean Christ's glory; and of course the Old Testament context is obviously Isaiah 6, the description of Isaiah's own commissioning.

Several questions confront one who looks at this chapter. What is the time element? Does the experience of chapter 6 follow chronologically the opening prophecies of chapters 1-5? What is the relationship of Isaiah's experience to the lifetime of King Uzziah? Where was Isaiah when he "saw the Lord" (v. 1)? Who are the seraphim? Those questions and others need to be considered.

It seems possible, perhaps likely, that in rounding out the opening section of God's indictment of Judah and Jerusalem Isaiah went back in time to that vision of the Lord that was the foundation of his ministry. One objection to that lies in the words of the opening verse of the book, which says that Isaiah prophesied during the reign of Uzziah and those of his three successors. However, the "year of King Uzziah's death" does not necessarily mean that the experience took place after Uzziah had died. In fact, it is much more likely that the well-known king was still living, but to die within the year; for if he had been dead already the prophet would more likely have dated the experience in the first year of Jotham. A very common interpretation asserts that Uzziah had already died and that the young Isaiah, who had perhaps put too much trust in the human ruler, now was able to get his eyes off the earthly king and see the heavenly King. That is reading into the passage something that is not necessarily there.

The prophet's awareness of his own sinfulness in itself is not proof of that position. Was Isaiah in the earthly Temple in Jerusalem or in a heavenly temple? Good commentators are found on each side of that question. If he were in the earthly Temple, does that mean he was a priest? Some of the prophets who were also priests made that fact known, notably Jeremiah and Ezekiel. There does not seem to be any indication that Isaiah was a priest. Might it not be that he went into the Temple court to worship, and that while he was there God gave him that supernatural glimpse of Himself? The Scripture is clear that no earthly building could possibly contain God (1 Kings 8:27; Acts 17:24). But in the theophanies God accommodated Himself in measure to the limitations of the beholders. Isaiah certainly could never forget that experience; he could never be in doubt about it; and would always remember when it occurred.

The overall impression conveyed by this vision is the glory and majesty of God as the exalted One. The sight of the throne emphasizes that God is the ruler and that He is in sovereign control. That is further emphasized by the word *Lord* (*Adonai*), which means the "sovereign Master." It is used again in verses 8 and 11. A different word—the name *Yahweh*—is used in verses 3, 5, and 12. It has already been pointed out that John refers to this experience as a view of Christ's glory. The Son of God is the revealer of God (John 1:18) before His incarnation as well as after.

The One whom Isaiah saw is the absolute Disposer of all events, the absolute Master of men. As so often in the Scriptures, His majesty and glory are set forth with a minimum of descriptive words, yet with a graphic power that causes us to see and to feel.

Who are the seraphim? They seem to be mentioned only here in the Scripture, although they bear some resemblance to the cherubim whom Ezekiel saw in his vision by the Chebar River (Ezek. 1:1-28 and 10:1-22), and to the four "living ones" John saw in his vision (Rev. 4:1—5:14). It is true that the same word is used for the fiery serpents in the experiences of Israel in the wilderness (Num. 21:6). The root word evidently means "to burn." They must be heavenly or angelic beings of a very high order, for they are around the throne of God and engage in continual praise of Him. They help to express the intense holiness of God to our feeble powers of perception. This is the supreme attribute of God—that He is separate from all that could defile. The Hebrew word for *holy* conveys the thought of absolute purity, of separation from all evil, of being set apart in His unique cleanness and effulgence.

Although the cherubim in Ezekiel and in Revelation (if they are the same as the four "living ones") are clearly specified as four in number, there is no indication here of how many seraphim there are. The Hebrew ending *-im*, of course, is the plural form. Those mighty creatures evidently burn in their ardor or zeal to honor and glorify God, who alone is worthy of praise. The covering of the faces seems to signify their reverence toward God. He had told Moses, "You cannot see My face, for no man can see Me and live!" (Ex. 33:20). The brilliance of God's glory that would be too much for a man to gaze on may even overwhelm a seraph (a "burning one").

The covering of the feet may indicate humility in service. Even the ministry of a seraph, completely holy and in unbroken submission to God, is not sufficient for His deserving. Hence, the seraphim acknowledge God's transcendence. It seems most likely that the seraphim are among the highest ranks of heavenly beings, not merely manifestations of God's attributes. Some who take the latter view think that would help to explain the statement that the seraphim stood "above" God (v. 2). It certainly could not mean that any created being is superior to the Creator! It evidently means that the seraphim are around God's throne in proximity to Him as they proclaim His dominant attribute. The Scripture indicates that there are different ranks or orders of heavenly beings both among the unfallen and the fallen. A reference to "thrones or dominions or rulers or authorities" is found in Colossians 1:16, for example.

The antiphonal cry of the seraphim celebrates God's holiness. Why do they proclaim that holiness three times?

Although some commentators doubt that there is an intimation of the Trinity here, it seems to be the most likely explanation. The seraphim do not praise God as twice holy or four times holy, but three times holy. In the light of the plain teaching of the New Testament on the Trinity, why should there be a problem in seeing foreshadows in the Old Testament? One must acknowledge that the full-fledged doctrine is not found in the Old Testament, but once the doctrine is seen as explicitly stated in the New Testament some of the otherwise hidden allusions of the Old Testament become understandable.

"The whole earth is full of His glory" (v. 3) may be an expression of its potential. Even in its sin-cursed state the earth is very beautiful and is a visible evidence of its Creator's existence and power (Rom. 1:20). Someday it will be completely delivered from the Adamic curse (Rom. 8:19-22). Eventually, redeemed mankind will join the inanimate creation in giving all praise and glory to God and the "earth will be full of the knowledge of the LORD as the waters cover the sea" (Isa. 11:9).

The voice of the seraph shook the building. The filling of the

Temple with smoke is reminiscent of other manifestations of God's glory, as when the Tabernacle was set up (Ex. 40:34-35) and at Solomon's dedication of the Temple (1 Kings 8:10-11).

Isaiah's whole prophetic ministry shows the effect of this experience. The expression "the Holy One of Israel," which is so much a characteristic of the book, arose from that event and was impressed indelibly on Isaiah's consciousness.

A vision of God gives a person a clear view of himself. It is very likely that Isaiah was an outstanding and exemplary young man, not a terrible sinner compared with other men. But it is often seen in the Scripture that those who are closest to God are the ones most aware of their own unworthiness. Today there seems to be an overemphasis on what is called a "good self-image." If that means that one denies his own sinfulness, then it is unscriptural, untrue, and unwholesome. If it means that one recognizes the grace of God which makes even the vilest sinner of infinite worth in God's sight (as evidenced by the death of the Lord Jesus), then we can accept the concept most gladly. There is absolutely no place for pride in the Christian life (1 Cor. 4:7).

Isaiah's experience was similar to that of others. Job, whom God Himself called a "blameless and upright man" (Job 1:8), was overwhelmed with a sense of his own worthlessness when he saw God. He said: "I have heard of thee by the hearing of the ear: but now mine eye seeth thee. Wherefore I abhor myself, and repent in dust and ashes" (Job 42:5-6, KJV).

Does that mean that Job's "friends" were right all along by calling him an outstanding sinner and a hypocrite? Of course not. It means that even one of the best men cannot compare himself with the infinitely holy God. Daniel, who is called by the angel Gabriel a "man greatly beloved" (Dan. 10:11, KJV), was overwhelmed by the vision he had of the glory of God (Dan. 10:15-17). He was prostrate and without strength. John, the "disciple whom Jesus loved" (John 21:20), when he saw the Lord Jesus in glorified appearance on the island of Patmos "fell at His feet as a dead man" (Rev. 1:17). All of those were exceptional men, among the best when compared with others.

Isaiah's experience was similar. "Woe is me," he cried out, "for I am ruined!" (v. 5). He was deeply conscious of the uncleanness of his person when compared with God's absolute holiness. He specifically mentioned his lips and the lips of the people among whom he lived, because they were not using their speech as the seraphim did to exalt and praise the "King, the LORD of hosts" (v. 5).

God had not brought Isaiah into this experience merely to let him despair. Isaiah's confession led to cleansing. It was only when he acknowledged his need that God met that need. That is a principle in salvation. Many people never get to the place where they will admit they have need of God's grace. The Lord Jesus said that He came not "to call the righteous, but sinners to repentance"(Matt. 9:13, KJV). Similarly, Christians often find their lives barren and fruitless because they will not or do not confess their sins. "If we confess our sins, he is faithful and just to forgive us our sins and to cleanse us from all unrighteousness" (1 John 1:9, KJV).

The live coal from the altar was the instrument of cleansing. Commentators differ about whether it is the altar of burnt offering or the golden altar of incense. In a number of places the Bible speaks of the cleansing effect of fire. The fire on the altar brings to mind the purifying judgment of God. Because the sacrificial system pointed forward to Christ, there is evidently a foreshadowing here of the cleansing that He provided by His death.

After the prophet's confession and cleansing came his commissioning by God. The coincidence of the King James Version helps one keep the order in memory: the "woe" of confession (v. 5) is followed by the "lo" of cleansing (v. 7), which leads to the "go" of commissioning (v. 9).

As previously indicated, this is probably not a re-commissioning but the account of Isaiah's original call, and thus out of order chronologically with the preceding prophecies. God prefers willing messengers, although in His sovereignty He can use even an unwilling one, such as Balaam (Num. 22:20). Consequently, God asked, "Whom shall I send, and who will go for Us?" (v. 8). Isaiah replied: "Here am I. Send me!"

God does not always give the same commission. Isaiah obviously was not to have an easy ministry. He was told before he began that the multitudes would not listen to him and that judgment would have to come on his people. But the situation was not completely hopeless. There would always be a "tenth portion" (v. 13). God always has His remnant, as the seven thousand in Elijah's day (1 Kings 19:18). Similarly, the apostle Paul could rejoice in his own day: "Even so . . . at this present time also there is a remnant according to the election of grace" (Rom. 11:5, KJV).

The comparatively small number who came back to the land with Zerubbabel after the Babylonian captivity could take comfort from that prophecy (Ezra 2:1-70).

2
The Book of Immanuel

(7:1 — 12:6)

One of the characteristics of predictive prophecy is the frequent mingling together of different times into a composite picture. The prophet must speak to his own time, of course, in a way that his contemporaries can understand. Nevertheless, he is not confined to his own time or even to the immediate future, for the Spirit of God bears him along to distant times and sometimes to distant places. The Holy Spirit especially brings to the attention of the prophet's hearers the times of the Messiah, the promised Redeemer. As has been shown, that is notably true of Isaiah.

Isaiah 7-12 is a section that aptly illustrates that principle. The prophecies were given during the reign of Ahaz (7:1) at a time when Syria and Israel were allied against Judah. The cowardly, paganized King Ahaz of Judah expected momentarily to be destroyed by those two enemy powers. Beyond that, the terrible might of the far larger and stronger Assyria threatened on the horizon. Through His prophet, God promises deliverance from those enemies but shows that the ultimate deliverance of His people can come only through the One whose name is Immanuel. In these chapters are some of the best-known prophecies of the Lord Jesus Christ. The section can be outlined in this way:

II. The Book of Immanuel (7:1—12:6)
   A. The Birth of Immanuel (7:1-17)
      1. Occasion of the Prophecy (7:1-9)
      2. The Sign to the House of David (7:10-17)

B. The Assyrian Invasion (7:18—8:22)
C. The Davidic Kingdom and King (9:1-7)
D. God's Stretched-out Hand of Judgment (9:8—10:34)
E. The Branch from Jesse's Roots (11:1-16)
F. The Song of Redemption (12:1-6)

THE BIRTH OF IMMANUEL (7:1-17)

After the kingdom was divided following the death of Solomon, the two resultant kingdoms were often at war with one another. The kingdom of Judah had the advantages of continuing under the Davidic dynasty and having the Temple with its attendant order of worship. In fact, many of the true believers who lived in Israel migrated into Judah to worship the Lord freely apart from the idolatrous practices introduced in Israel by Jeroboam I (2 Chron. 11:16).

As the Northern Kingdom became more and more corrupt, it eventually came to the sad condition mentioned here, in which one group of the people united with a pagan foreign power against the other group—"Syria is confederate with Ephraim" (v. 2, KJV). The name *Ephraim* was sometimes used for the Northern Kingdom because of the dominant place of the tribe of Ephraim in that nation (see Hos. 11:8).

Terror spread from King Ahaz throughout the populace. In the midst of that panic Isaiah, the prophet of God, set out at God's command to meet Ahaz, taking with him his son whose symbolic name was *Shear-jashub* ("a remnant shall return" [7:3]).

God's assurance and the stability that it engendered came in the midst of human confusion: "Thus says the Lord GOD, 'It shall not stand nor shall it come to pass'" (v. 7).

The historical circumstances mentioned in this paragraph form the background of the prophet's triumphant announcement to Ahaz and lead into one of the most remarkable of all prophecies—the virgin birth of Christ (see 2 Kings 16:5). During his reign Uzziah had taken Elath from Damascene Syria (Hebrew, *Aram*). Syria was now trying to avenge previous calamities and recover previous losses (cf. 2 Kings 14:22). Rezin, the king of Aram, formed an alliance with the usurper Pekah, son of Remaliah, the king of Israel (2 Kings 15:25). The invasion mentioned in this passage was probably in the first year of the reign of Ahaz.

The army of Ahaz was destroyed (2 Chron. 28:5-15), but the allied enemies were not able to conquer Jerusalem (2 Kings 16:7-9).

The words of Isaiah to King Ahaz were delivered between the first successes of the enemy powers and their final retreat. In verse 2, which precedes verse 1 chronologically, the "house of David" refers to the government of which Ahaz was the head.

Isaiah warned the king against acting in self-will apart from God's leading and exhorted him to have a calmness that could come only from confidence in God. Calvin comments that God exhorted him "to restrain himself outwardly, and keep his mind calm within."[1]

The enemies are presented as God sees them, not worthy of consideration. "They were two tails," the ends of "wooden pokers . . . which would not blaze any more, but only continue smoking."[2] No matter how powerful those foes might seem to be, they could not alter the course of history as ordained by God. The ten-tribe kingdom, whose alliance with Syria was ungodly and unnatural, was to cease to exist as a nation within sixty-five years (v. 8). The Assyrian conquest of Samaria came much sooner than that, but apparently the period of sixty-five years covers the time until the beginning of Ashurbanipal's reign in 669 B.C., at which time the Assyrian ruler completed the transportation of people of other nations to Samaria, which had been begun by Esarhaddon (cf. Ezra 4:2, 10). By that date the Northern Kingdom had been effectively wiped out. The sixty-five years would include fourteen of Ahaz, twenty-nine of Hezekiah, and twenty-two of Manasseh.

The announcement of Israel's fall is accompanied by a warning to Judah that if it acts like Israel it also will perish. There is paronomasia in the words *believe* and *last* (*be established*, KJV); they are variant forms from the same verb root (v. 9).

The Lord's instruction to Ahaz to ask for a sign may have come on a later occasion or later on this same occasion. The latter seems preferable.

The term *sign* (v. 11) indicates a visible pledge of the truth of something that confirms a given word. The sign is sometimes a

1. John Calvin, *Commentary on the Book of Isaiah*, 1:232.
2. Franz Delitzsch, *Biblical Commentary on the Prophecies of Isaiah*, 1:209.

miracle (Ex. 4:8), sometimes a prediction (Ex. 3:12), and sometimes a symbol (Isa. 8:18). Here the sign is a miraculous event that shows that the prediction will come true. The prediction is that the alliance will be broken and that the nation will not be overrun at that time.

The language with which the Lord gives the instruction to ask for a sign shows that it was to be no ordinary occurrence: "Make it deep as Sheol or high as heaven" (v. 11). That transcends any prosaic or pedestrian event. Franz Delitzsch has a good section here in which he ridicules the perplexity of rationalistic commentators over this passage. Quoting Meier to the effect that Isaiah did not intend to perform an actual miracle, Delitzsch shrewdly observes, "Probably because no miracle was ever performed by Goethe, to whose high poetic consecration Meier compares the consecration of the prophet as described in ch. vi." His conclusion of the argument is excellent.

> Dazzled by the glory of the Old Testament prophecy, a rationalistic exegesis falls prostrate upon the ground; and it is with such frivolous, coarse and common words as these that it tries to escape from its difficulties. It cannot acknowledge the miraculous power of the prophet, because it believes in no miracles at all.[3]

Ahaz, whose character is well known (2 Kings 16:2-4), gives a hypocritical answer. In a sanctimonious way he apparently invokes the command of Deuteronomy 6:16—"You shall not put the LORD your God to the test." With a pretense of piety "in order to avoid being disturbed in his Assyrian policy" (Delitzsch), Ahaz was seeking the help of Assyria to defeat his more immediate enemies even while he spoke. What a fatuous policy it was to depend on the cruel and aggressive Assyrian nation for help. Assyria "helped" smaller nations by absorbing them and destroying their identity. In the situation in which Ahaz found himself, he was like a mouse being attacked by two rats and asking the cat for help.

Through Isaiah, God speaks to the whole house of David, not just to King Ahaz (v. 13). Because the king had rejected God, Isaiah does not say "*your* God"; instead he says "*my* God." Because Ahaz would not choose, the Lord Himself acted and gave

3. Ibid., p. 215.

him a sign (v. 14). It was not to Ahaz alone (in which case the singular pronoun would have been used) but to the Davidic dynasty; hence the plural. To even imply that doing what God commanded with regard to the sign would be tempting Him exposes the extraordinary wickedness and folly of Ahaz.

Much speculation and controversy have surrounded the prophecy of Isaiah 7:14. There is much questioning about the meaning of "the virgin" (*ha almah*) and the identity of the baby who is to be born. It does not seem at all likely that it could be a reference to Isaiah's wife, who is called in 8:3 "the prophetess." Usage is in favor of rendering *almah* as a marriageable virgin. In addition to this passage, the word occurs six times in the Old Testament: Genesis 24:43; Exodus 2:8; Psalm 68:26; Song of Solomon 1:3 and 6:8; and Proverbs 30:19. It also occurs in the masculine form in 1 Samuel 17:56 and 20:22.

The New Testament translates that passage and uses the Greek word *parthenos,* which can mean nothing else but "virgin" (Matt. 1:23).

There are three major views about the identity of the "son" mentioned in the passage.

1. According to some interpreters the narrative relates the birth and infancy of a child born in the ordinary course of nature during Isaiah's lifetime. That is, the word *almah* simply means a young woman of marriageable age who is a virgin prior to the conception of that child. One difficulty with that view is that it does not seem to be a sign of the magnitude demanded by the context. It would certainly not be unique for a young woman to bear a son. In what way would that express a miracle that would constitute a sign to the whole house of David?

   This view would seem to be contrary to the normal usage of *almah* in the Hebrew Old Testament. Another objection is the parallel passage in Isaiah 9:6-7, where the child who is born is described in terms of deity. Furthermore, the use made of the passage in the New Testament seems to be against such a limited interpretation. There the word *parthenos* does not mean a young woman who was a virgin before the conception of her child, but one who was still a virgin at the time the child was born. In any case, Isaiah's wife could not fit that description because she already had at least one child, Shear-jashub, who is specifically mentioned in the context.

The other two views both see the prophecy as linked in some way to the virgin birth of Christ. There are good interpreters who hold either of those views. Both see a messianic element, but the difference of opinion is whether the prophecy is *exclusively* messianic.

2. A second view is that the prophecy has a double meaning and refers to two distinct births. The primary sense tells of the birth of a child in the ordinary course of nature; but the terms are so chosen as to be descriptive of the miraculous birth of Christ. In this case, the nearness of the birth would be a sign to Ahaz and would point forward to the birth of the Messiah.

Those who hold that view compare this passage to Hosea 11:1: "When Israel was a youth I loved him, and out of Egypt I called My son." In the context that evidently refers to the nation of Israel. However, the New Testament shows that it is in some sense a prophecy of Christ:

And he arose and took the Child and His mother by night, and departed for Egypt; and was there until the death of Herod, that what was spoken by the Lord through the prophet might be fulfilled, saying, "Out of Egypt did I call My Son." [Matt. 2:14-15]

That interpretation certainly fits into the context and does not do violence to the New Testament usage, for it fully accepts the virgin birth of Christ. One seeming objection to the view is its complexity, and in the opinion of some its probability is further decreased by the lack of similarity in the two postulated events. In its primary sense it may not give a sufficient sign as demanded by the context. This view sees the sign as being not just the birth, but the time that was necessary for the young boy to be able to choose between good and evil. Thus the sign is the destruction of the Syrio-Israelite alliance within the next five or six years.

3. The third view is that the passage is definitely and exclusively messianic, although this interpretation is not without its difficulties. One of the most serious objections is that the far-away virgin birth could not be a sign to Ahaz, since there would be no fulfillment in his time.

A possible answer to that objection is that the virgin birth was not given as a sign to Ahaz alone, but to the whole house of David which Ahaz represented, however poorly, in his generation.

But this prophecy seems to be like some others that give a glimpse of messianic times without giving an indication of the length of time involved before the events take place. According to this particular view, there is contingency in the passage. The thought seems to be that if the young Immanuel were born immediately, then before he would be old enough to discern between good and evil the land would be delivered from its oppressors. In that sense there is in the prophecy both a message for the age and the ages. Ahaz was given the assurance that the Syrio-Israelite invasion would not prevail, and the "house of David" had the greater assurance of the great deliverer, Immanuel.

According to either of the first two views, the baby in Ahaz's day would have borne the name *Immanuel* in a symbolic sense, just as the Old Testament leader Joshua bore the name that in its fullest sense belongs to the New Testament "Joshua," the Lord Jesus Christ. The name would be an assurance from the Lord, for it means "God with us."

The third view (the exclusively messianic interpretation) sees the name given only to the Lord Jesus, not in a merely figurative way as a testimony that God is with us, but in the most literal way as the One who is, as God Himself, actually with us in the sense of becoming one of us. This great prophetic name of the Lord Jesus sets forth both His deity and His humanity. This is similar to the statement of the apostle John: "And the Word became flesh, and dwelt among us, and we beheld His glory, glory as of the only begotten from the Father, full of grace and truth" (John 1:14). The great Christological passage in Philippians 2:5-11 is an apt commentary on this name of our wonderful Lord.

THE ASSYRIAN INVASION (7:18—8:22)

The prophet goes on to show Ahaz that Assyria, on which he was relying, would come on Judah in a more devastating invasion than that of Syria and Israel (7:20). The country Ahaz had appealed to out of fear of Syria and Israel would itself bring Judah into most serious trouble.

The name of Isaiah's son prophesied the nearness of the fall of Israel and Syria (8:1-4). Isaiah wrote out the message on a large tablet: *Maher-shalal-hash-baz*, "swift is the booty, speedy is the prey." The two witnesses (v. 2) attested to the fact that Isaiah's message was true. This idea of two witnesses was from the law (Num. 35:30; Deut. 17:6; 19:15). The text records that Isaiah's son was born and that before he could utter the words "father" or "mother" the alliance would fall. In other words, the alliance would fall within about two years of the time that Isaiah first gave the message—nine months for the birth and then one year before the baby could speak.

Ahaz had been concerned with the Israel-Syria alliance. But now Isaiah prophesied of the real danger—the invasion by Assyria. He noted that judgment was going to come on Israel because of its rejection of the Southern Kingdom and all that it stood for. Not only would the invasion sweep through the Northern Kingdom, but it would also come down all the way into Judah, called here the land of Immanuel (v. 8).

In spite of the alliance, which was against them at this time, Isaiah affirmed that the ultimate victory would be with the people of God (vv. 9-15). No matter how great a confederation of enemies there may be, God will deliver His people if they look to Him. They need not fear the hostile coalitions if they are reverencing their God. "And He shall be your fear, and He shall be your dread" (v. 13). The lesson is repeated often in Scripture that trust in God drives out the fear of man or of the devil. The alliance will be shattered because God is with Jerusalem (vv. 9-10). "God is with us" (v. 10) is once again Immanuel. The people could take heart that they were in a covenant relationship with the God who was with them. However, because of this relationship the people were to fear God, not the alliance that threatened them (vv. 11-15).

In this context Isaiah spoke of himself and his children as set for "signs and wonders in Israel" (v. 18). It was noted earlier that Isaiah himself had a symbolic name indicating the almighty power of God in salvation to the ends of the earth. Likewise, his two sons were given symbolic names: Shear-jashub and Maher-shalal-hash-baz.

Isaiah—"the salvation of Yahweh"

Maher-shalal-hash-baz—"swift is the booty, speedy is the prey"

Shear-jashub—"a remnant will return"

Isaiah noted that the nation was to consult the word of the Lord, not mediums and spiritists who cannot deliver the nation. Once again Isaiah is reminding the people of the Deuteronomic covenant. It promised peace and prosperity as long as the people were living according to the word of God, but also promised them destruction and captivity if they departed from that word and the covenantal stipulations. It is God alone who can bring deliverance for the nation, not false teachers and false prophets who turn the people to false gods.

THE DAVIDIC KINGDOM AND KING (9:1-7)

At the opening of chapter 9 the prophecy takes a tremendous leap across the centuries. In fact, there are two leaps, for both advents of the Lord Jesus Christ are in view.

The New Testament makes clear that this prophecy was partially fulfilled by the ministry of our Lord in Galilee at His first coming (cf. Isa. 9:1-2 with Matt. 4:13-16).

It is obvious, however, that not everything in the prophecy was fulfilled at that time. As in a number of other Old Testament passages, the two comings of Christ are brought together in one prophecy. The Old Testament prophet, standing far off from what God allowed him to see, perceived two great mountain peaks as if they were only one. He could not see the valley between the peaks—the present age between the two advents of Christ.

We who live in that valley can look back on our Lord's first coming and forward to His second coming. Through God's grace New Testament believers have a marvelous advantage that even the greatest of God's servants in Old Testament times did not have. Peter tells of the perplexity of the Old Testament prophets as they reviewed their own writings, which the Holy Spirit had given them by inspiration:

As to this salvation, the prophets who prophesied of the grace that would come to you made careful search and inquiry, seeking to know what person or time the Spirit of Christ within them was indicating as He predicted the sufferings of Christ and the glories to follow. [1 Pet. 1:10-11]

How wonderful to remember that our Lord graciously fulfilled part of this prophecy as He ministered in Galilee. Many people in that area received the "great light" (v. 2) of His presence as He "went about doing good" (Acts 10:38).

The birth of the child prophesied in Isaiah 9:6 has occurred long ago, at Christ's first coming. His universal reign has not yet been fulfilled; that awaits His return. The two natures of Christ in one perfect Person are indicated by the terms of the prophecy: "a child is born"—that is His genuine humanity; "a son is given"—that is His absolute deity. Lest there be any doubt, He is given titles that no mere man could have.

In Scripture names often have meaning. When Scripture says what the name of this person is, that indicates what He really is; that is, His character.

In the current scene people are prone to exaggerate in their assessment of other people and things. In the commercial realm one's product is always better than others' products. Indeed, it is always better than it was formerly, since it has been improved! On the political scene one party's candidate is always the greatest and the best, but so is the other party's candidate.

But here is a Person concerning whom no one could possibly exaggerate, because anything that could be said of the Lord Jesus falls short of the reality of His Person.

There is a difference of opinion among commentators whether this glorious name consists of four or five elements. A number of the widely used modern versions punctuate it as four parts, linking the words *Wonderful Counselor* together. One argument for this view is that there are then four nouns, each with its accompanying adjective: "Wonderful Counselor, Mighty God, Eternal Father, Prince of Peace" (NASB).

Others take the terms to be five in number: "Wonderful, Counselor, the Mighty God, Everlasting Father, the Prince of Peace" (KJV). The word *Wonderful*, according to this interpretation, stands alone as a comprehensive description of the Lord Jesus Christ in His Person and work. This is similar to what He said of Himself as the Angel of the Lord (Yahweh) in appearing to the parents of Samson (Judg. 13:18).

The Lord Jesus is wonderful in His Person because He is unique. There is no one else like Him, for He is the God-Man. Even among the Persons of the Godhead He is unique, for neither the Father nor the Holy Spirit became incarnate; only the Son did. The Father's delight is in Him, and the Holy Spirit's work is to glorify Him (Isa. 42:1; Matt. 3:17; 17:5; John 16:14).

Furthermore, our Lord is wonderful in His work. He did that which no one else could do. The psalmist said of all men that no one could redeem his brother or "give to God a ransom for him" (Ps. 49:7). The writer to the Hebrews declares that "when he had by himself purged our sins, [He] sat down on the right hand of the Majesty on high" (Heb. 1:3, KJV). He Himself said, "For even the Son of Man did not come to be served, but to serve, and to give His life a ransom for many" (Mark 10:45).

The Scripture says that in Christ are hidden "all the treasures of wisdom and knowledge" (Col. 2:3). No wonder that His name is *Counselor*. Human counselors are limited in various ways. Some have knowledge but lack compassion. Some are full of compassion but limited in knowledge. But the Lord Jesus Christ is the omniscient One and the compassionate One. "And seeing the multitudes, He felt compassion for them, because they were distressed and downcast like sheep without a shepherd" (Matt. 9:36). His title *Mighty God* denotes His almighty power manifested in creation and available to His people. The Hebrew *el-gibbor* cannot be vitiated to mean a god-hero in the fashion of the pagan demigods. It must signify absolute deity, which is already implied in the context as can be seen by the parallelism in the verse. It is also parallel to the prophecy in 7:14.

The title *Eternal Father* is perhaps the most perplexing of the whole series, because it is normally applied to the first Person of the Godhead. The One described here is obviously the second Person, the One known in the New Testament as the Lord Jesus Christ. One must not confuse the Persons of the Godhead as the ancient heretics the Patripassians did, of whom Tertullian charged that they "put to flight the Paraclete, and . . . crucified the Father."[4] The Father is not the Son and the Son is not the Father,

4. *Against Praxeas*, "The Ante-Nicene Fathers," ed. Alexander Roberts and James Donaldson (Buffalo: Christian Literature, 1885), 3:597.

although the Father is God and the Son is God (the very same God).

This expression in the text being considered is not intended to describe Trinitarian distinctions, but to stress the everlasting care that the Lord Jesus gives to His own. He is literally "the Father of eternity," the One who nourishes and protects His own forever. As a human father is supposed to provide security for his family, so the Lord Jesus lovingly provides for His own throughout all ages. The *Prince of Peace* in the immediate context is the One who brings peace to the war-ravaged world through His presence and reign. This is a foregleam of the millennial kingdom celebrated so often in the Prophets. His kingdom with its resultant peace will continue perpetually (v. 7). To affirm its certainty God makes the statement, "The zeal of the LORD of hosts will accomplish this," a statement that occurs in only two other places in Scripture (2 Kings 19:31 and Isa. 37:32).

Those who do not take prophetic passages literally have no explanation for the emphasis in Scripture that the Lord Jesus will reign on the throne of David. If His kingdom is not a literal, earthly kingdom but only a spiritualized expression, what would be the need of His descent from David? The Davidic Covenant (2 Sam. 7:1-29) is a clear and unconditional promise from God that David will never lack a man to sit on his throne. The throne of David is real and literal.

That is not only stressed in the Old Testament but in the New Testament as well. The angel Gabriel told Mary, "The Lord God will give Him the throne of His father David; and He will reign over the house of Jacob forever; and His kingdom will have no end" (Luke 1:32-33). In using the name *Jacob* (instead of *Israel*) the Scriptures seem to be emphasizing the literalness of this prophecy.

The New Testament begins with Christ's official descent from David (Matt. 1:1), and Paul opens the epistle to the Romans with a reminder of Christ's relationship to David (Rom. 1:3).

GOD'S STRETCHED-OUT HAND OF JUDGMENT (9:8—10:34)

The stretched-out hand of God is seen repeatedly in this section (see 9:12, 17, 21; 10:4; cf. also 5:25). It is not a display of mercy, as in some other places where God is seen as stretching out the hand of grace toward the sinner, but an indication of judgment. Because

God's previous judgments have not had the desired effect of turning His people to repentance (9:13), He must continue to smite them.

God used the wicked nation of Assyria to punish His own people for their sins (10:5). That is the lesson the prophet Habakkuk learned later in his perplexity about God's using wicked Babylon to punish wicked Judah (Hab. 1:12—2:20). How can God do that and keep everything in perfect balance? Because He is omniscient and omnipotent. That may be paradoxical to us, but not a problem with God. The psalmist said, "For the wrath of man shall praise Thee" (Ps. 76:10).

But God will not allow Assyria to escape His righteous judgment either. Men delude themselves into thinking they are going their own way, declaring their independence from God. The powerful nation of Assyria was serving a divine purpose as a tool in the hand of the Lord. That did not by any means excuse Assyria's actions or absolve it of its guilt.

So it will be that when the Lord has completed all His work on Mount Zion and on Jerusalem, He will say, "I will punish the fruit of the arrogant heart of the king of Assyria and the pomp of his haughtiness." [10:12]

God's sovereignty and man's responsibility are always in perfect balance in the Word of God. Even though one is not able to reconcile that antinomy, one can believe both parts of it because the Bible clearly teaches both parts. God is sovereign in His universe; at the same time man is fully accountable to God for all his acts.

The reference to "that day" (10:20) seems to carry the prophecy over from the historical invasion in the prophet's time to another tremendous invasion of the land in the end time. Whatever the exact connection may be, the sequel in chapter 11 would seem to indicate such a far view. The "shoot . . . from the stem of Jesse" (11:1) can only be the Messiah.

THE BRANCH FROM JESSE'S ROOTS (11:1-16)

How exquisitely the Lord Jesus Christ is portrayed in the writings of the "evangelical prophet"! In 11:1 He is characterized again as the "branch," although the Hebrew word used here is not the same as in 4:2. He is seen as the true successor of David—as the Messiah-King. The description of His enduement by the Spirit of God is in keeping with the New Testament statement that "God giveth not the Spirit by measure unto him" (John 3:34, KJV).

In chapter nine there is an emphasis on the peace that will attend His reign (9:7). In this passage the stress is on the righteousness that will characterize His kingdom (cf. Ps. 85:10, where righteousness and peace are seen in perfect harmony in Messiah's reign). Men desire peace, but they do not have as great a desire for righteousness. No ordinary or even extraordinary man could reign in perfect righteousness; only the God-Man can do that (cf. Isa. 32:1).

The description in verse 2 of the Spirit's resting on Him, which is given in a sevenfold way, is probably the source of that striking figure in the book of Revelation where the "seven Spirits of God" are mentioned (Rev. 1:4; 3:1). Seven is used symbolically in various parts of the Scripture to denote divine completeness or divine perfection. The seven Spirits of God seem to be the Holy Spirit in all the fullness and perfection of His Person and power, or as already indicated, the Spirit not given by measure; that is, not limited in any way.

The Lord Jesus Christ's absolute "fairness" (v. 4) ought to be a source of consolation. There is so much now that is unfair. Even those who try to be fair are often unfair because of some limitation of knowledge or ability. That fairness, however, demands judgment on sinners and punishment for their sin. The "rod of His mouth" (v. 4) is parallel to the statement in Psalm 2, where the Messiah is told by God the Father, "Thou shalt break them with a rod of iron; thou shalt dash them in pieces like a potter's vessel" (Ps. 2:9, KJV). There is an echo of this passage also in Revelation 19:15.

Through verse 5 most evangelical commentators will probably agree. But when the prophecy begins to describe changed conditions within the animal creation, there comes a divergence of views. Many refuse to take this part literally, evidently because such acceptance would involve changes in the course of what is called "nature." Many are disposed to allegorize or spiritualize the Old Testament prophecies concerning the kingdom. Fulfilled prophecy, however, furnishes a standard by which to interpret prophecy that has not yet been fulfilled. If the prophecies concerning the sufferings of Christ were fulfilled generally in a literal manner, should it not be expected that the prophecies concerning His glory will be similarly fulfilled?

No one can deny that there are many figures of speech in prophetic passages; nor can God describe the coming glory in a way that we can completely understand. But if kingdom prophecy means anything, it means that a day will come when Christ shall personally and literally reign over this earth. This messianic reign is often referred to as the millennium, based on the passage concerning the thousand years in Revelation 20.

That prophecy in Revelation is the culmination and climax of a great number of prophecies in the Old and New Testaments concerning the future reign of the Messiah.

The New Testament declares that eventually the material creation is to be delivered from the bondage into which it came because of Adam's sin (Rom. 8:19-22). It is not heaven that is being described in this passage; it is Christ's coming kingdom on the earth. Consequently, when the text mentions wolves, lambs, leopards, kids, and so on, it is referring to those literal animals, not just a fanciful, ethereal scene in some "never-never" land. It reflects a basic change in the nature of animals. The struggle for existence that is so often talked about will then have ceased. "The wolf will dwell with the lamb. . . . And a little boy will lead them" (v. 6). Ferocious and carnivorous beasts will become gentle, tractable, and herbivorous: "the lion will eat straw like the ox" (v. 7). Why should one look for a so-called "spiritual" explanation of those words when they are perfectly clear taken literally?

Some who will not accept such a passage literally probably do not accept the historicity and literalness of the Genesis record that tells of the entrance of sin into the world. When one will not accept the plain statements of Scripture at face value, one tends to become enmeshed in an evergrowing web of evasion.

This brief picture in Isaiah 11 shows something of the coming glory of that future day: "They will not hurt or destroy in all My holy mountain, for the earth will be full of the knowledge of the LORD as the waters cover the sea" (v.9).

In the verses that follow, that coming deliverance of God's people is compared to the ancient deliverance from Egypt. This time they will be coming from all over the earth (v. 12). The "remnant" (vv. 11 and 16) and the "highway" (v. 16) are two of the leading motifs in Isaiah. The "highway" finds later echoes (35:8; 40:3). Such a use of recurring themes is one of the evidences of the authorship and unity of the book.

Assyria is specifically mentioned (v. 16), and that is significant because the underlying historical setting for these chapters (7-12) is the Assyrian invasions, in one of which Israel was conquered, and another in which Judah was to be very seriously threatened.

THE SONG OF REDEMPTION (12:1-6)

The "book of Immanuel" closes with a lovely song. In the opening section the birth of Immanuel was announced (7:14). That was against the tragic background of foreign invasions, at first that of Syria and Israel, and later, that of Assyria. The prophecy moves back and forth between the near view and the far view. The godly remnant are seen in that coming day (v. 1), the day of salvation for the nation (cf. Rom. 11:26).

The song is in two parts: verses 1-2 and verses 3-6. The first part looks back on the judgment of God and then rests in His comfort (cf. 40:1). It acknowledges God as "strength," "song," and "salvation."

The second part is a pure hymn of praise, celebrating "the Holy One of Israel" in the midst of His people (v. 6).

"I will trust and not be afraid" (v. 2) is the response of the true believer. Drawing "water from the springs of salvation" (v. 3) is a refreshing and meaningful allusion often found in Scripture (cf. Isa. 55:1; Ps. 42:1; John 4:13-14; Rev. 22:17). The conclusion of the song is similar to the last statement in the book of Ezekiel where the name of the city is given as "The LORD is there" (Ezek. 48:35).

God's Word has a universal applicability, although one must be careful not to confuse application with primary interpretation. Even though this song will find its true setting in the coming kingdom age, any believer in any age can sing, "I will trust and not be afraid (v. 2)."

3

The Burdens on the Nations

(13:1 — 23:18)

Chapters 13-23 contain a series of messages primarily directed against various Gentile nations, especially those surrounding and touching the life of Judah. Both the *New American Standard Bible* and the *New International Version* use the word *oracle* as the title of each of those messages. The NASB has a marginal note: "lit., *burden.*" The King James Version translates the term as "burden" and attaches it to each of the messages. The term in question is derived from a word that denotes something heavy, and thus came to have the connotations of "burden" and "an important utterance." The emphasis in the prophecies is judgment—thus they were important or weighty and should be considered carefully by the surrounding nations and by the nation of Israel.

Actually, it is unlikely that Isaiah intended for the foreign nations to read of the judgments of Yahweh upon them. His intent was primarily to provide a prophetic hope for the nation of Israel. The hope would be immediate for the recipients of the divinely given messages in Isaiah's day and would be observable by future generations as those prophecies of doom and destruction came to pass.

Each of the three great prophetical books—Isaiah, Jeremiah, and Ezekiel—contains a list of judgments or oracles against the nations. When the three prophets are compared (Isa. 13-23; Jer. 46-51; Ezek. 25-32) the lists of oracles look as follows:

Isaiah	Jeremiah	Ezekiel
Babylon	Egypt	Ammon
Philistia	Philistia	Moab
Moab	Moab	Edom
Damascus (Syria)	Ammon	Philistia
Cush/Ethiopia	Edom	Tyre
Egypt	Damascus	Sidon
Negev	Kedar/Hazor	Egypt
Edom/Dumah	Elam	
Arabia	Babylon	
Jerusalem (Valley of Vision)		
Tyre		

In both Isaiah and Jeremiah, Babylon is the empire emphasized for judgment. In Ezekiel, Egypt bears the full force of the judgmental oracle. In Isaiah, Babylon is standing at the top of the list and at the height of Yahweh's destructive force. The fall of Babylon, which is often seen in Scripture as the arch-enemy of God and His people, is presented as something that should cause all the people of God to rejoice.

In his oracles of judgment Isaiah moves from Babylon westward to Tyre (in contrast to Jeremiah who begins with Egypt and moves eastward to Babylon). In the oracles, Isaiah uses much figurative language to describe the ultimate judgment of the various nations.

The section can be outlined as follows:

III. The Burdens on the Nations (13:1—23:18)
    A. The Burden of Babylon (13:1—14:27)
    B. The Burden of Philistia (14:28-32)
    C. The Burden of Moab (15:1—16:14)
    D. The Burden of Damascus (Syria) (17:1-14)
    E. The Burden of Cush (Ethiopia) (18:1-7)
    F. The Burden of Egypt (19:1—20:6)
    G. The Burden of the Wilderness of the Sea (Negev) (21:1-10)
    H. The Burden of Edom/Dumah (21:11-12)
    I. The Burden of Arabia (21:13-17)
    J. The Burden of Jerusalem (22:1-25)
    K. The Burden of Tyre (23:1-18).

The prophecies are of unequal length and many of the terms are difficult to interpret. Much effort is needed to link the events in these chapters with events recorded elsewhere in Scripture and events found in the historical records.

Before looking at the individual oracles it is necessary to look at two general principles that permeate the section.

One such principle is God's absolute and holy justice. God will hold every nation or people accountable for its actions. Regardless of the availability of revelations, all nations are required to conform to God's standards.

The other principle is the place of prophecy as the confirmation of God's Word. The fact that the nations of ancient times met their individual destinies as predicted in the Bible is corroborative evidence that the Bible is in truth the Word of God. It would have been a relatively easy matter for Israelites living in the time of the return to the land under Zerubbabel, Ezra, and Nehemiah to look back at the prophecies of Isaiah concerning the empires in existence in his time (c. 700 B.C.) and to see whether or not God had spoken through him.

THE ORACLE CONCERNING BABYLON (13:1—14:27)

The oracle concerning Babylon can be divided into four parts. Isaiah first noted the fall of Babylon (13:1-16). He next prophesied that the Medes were to be the agents who toppled the great empire of Babylon (13:17-22). He then predicted a time when Israel would find itself again in the land, settled and ruling over the peoples who had oppressed them (14:1-2). Finally, he went into great detail in speaking of the destruction of the king of Babylon (14:3-27).

It is particularly fitting that the oracle against Babylon should stand first in Isaiah's list. From its very beginning Babylon had been the rallying point of rebellion against God in the period shortly after the flood (Gen. 11:1-9). In many places in the Old Testament Babylon represents the idolatrous pagan world system that stands in opposition to God. Although various dynasties and empires flourished in Babylon, it was constantly seen by Israel as a city that hated the God of Israel. That symbolism is carried over into the New Testament in the book of Revelation.

Since Isaiah's prophecy is so largely concerned with the coming of the Babylonian captivity of Judah, it is most fitting that God's people know ahead of time that their powerful enemy will eventually meet its doom. Much is said about the destruction of Babylon and its idols in the second part of Isaiah.

It is interesting that some of those who hold that the second part of the book was not written by Isaiah also question the authenticity of this section in spite of the fact that Isaiah's name is specifically attached to it (13:1).

The fulfillment was to come about through the conquest of Babylon by the Medes and the Persians almost two centuries after Isaiah's time (prophesied in chapters 44 and 45, where Cyrus the Persian, the general of the invading forces, is mentioned specifically as the deliverer of the people of Judah from Babylon). The prophecy also looks forward by analogy to the end time, for the expression "the Day of the LORD" normally indicates the future time of God's direct intervention in judgment into human affairs. The term has great eschatological significance.

The view has been widely held that the city of Babylon on the Euphrates will be rebuilt in the end time as the great world capital of the Antichrist. Those who hold that view assert that Isaiah's prophecy of the complete destruction of Babylon has not been fulfilled because the city still existed long after the time of the Persian conquest. But as many have shown, Babylon's decline was gradual. The geographer Strabo (about 20 B.C.) spoke of the site of Babylon as a "vast desolation." In the light of Isaiah's prophecy that Babylon will not be rebuilt or inhabited (13:19-22), it seems more likely that "Babylon" in Revelation is not Babylon on the Euphrates but symbolic Babylon, represented in the end time by the Roman Empire. The city in Revelation fits what is known of the city of Rome better than it does the historical Babylon.

THE FALL OF BABYLON (13:1-16)

In this section the prophet gives an overview of what will happen to the mighty Babylonian Empire, which was dreaded by the entire world. It is important to remember that at the time this section was written Babylon was not a dreaded empire. Assyria was still the empire in power in the Near East. Babylon was a city within the Assyrian Empire that had had a long history of revolt, and was finally crushed in 689 B.C. Even after that defeat the city of Babylon was restored and once again became a magnificent city.

Because of the mention of Assyria in 14:24-27 it seems likely that Isaiah is writing of the Assyrian Empire, using Babylon as a symbol of all the anti-God forces. Babylon was not the capital of the Assyrian Empire but a major city within the reach of the empire. Isaiah spoke against Babylon because of the important anti-God role that it would play later in Israel's history. Perhaps the imagery for the section was the Assyrian invasion into Judah under Sennacherib, possibly in 701 B.C. Thus Isaiah's symbolism of the nations coming to battle (vv. 4-5) could speak of the Assyrian invasion, but be prophetic of that great conflict that will occur in the campaign of Armageddon. Isaiah describes what will happen when the armies realize that the Lord and His armies are coming in triumph (vv. 6-9). The people who dare to fight against the Lord will be utterly defeated and terrified. There will be great changes occurring on the earth during the time of the great judgment of God (vv. 10-16).

THE MEDES WILL DEFEAT BABYLON (13:17-22)

Some have wondered about the inclusion of these verses concerning the victory of the Medes over Babylon. It is well known that the Medes were active against the Assyrians during a long power struggle. Ultimately it was the Medes who defeated and conquered Nineveh (612 B.C.). Eventually the Medo-Persian armies conquered Babylon under the leadership of Cyrus, but the city was governed by Darius the Mede. Isaiah seems to be telescoping all the events together, culminating them in the fall of the city of Babylon (539 B.C.).

A TIME OF PROSPERITY (14:1-2)

Isaiah wants to be very clear that the defeat of Babylon has eschatological overtones; he wants the readers to understand that he is ultimately speaking of the millennial kingdom that will be brought in for Israel. It is significant that he uses the terms *Israel* and *Jacob* in speaking of the nation, for he prophesied a reunited kingdom ruling in power again as it had in the days of David and Solomon. Isaiah notes a complete reversal of position. Israel, which had been the captive, the one subject to the rulership of Assyria, will in that day be the captors while Assyria and the nations will be Israel's servants.

DESTRUCTION OF THE KING OF BABYLON (14:3-27)

The "taunt" (v. 4) recorded by Isaiah has been variously interpreted over the years. The main issue in the interpretation is the phrase "the king of Babylon." A number of interpretations have been offered. Perhaps the one most widely held is that Isaiah is prophetically speaking of the fall of Nebuchadnezzar, who was the epitome of a Babylonian king in all of his pride and arrogance. Scripture itself mentions that he was eventually brought low (Dan. 4:1-18).

A second view is that Isaiah is speaking of the Assyrian kings who ruled over Babylon at the time of Isaiah. This view stems primarily from verses 24-27 where the Lord vows to break Assyria (v. 25). It has been pointed out that Pul (2 Kings 15:19), also known as Tiglath-pileser, was the king of Babylon and may be the prototype in Isaiah's day of an arrogant, proud king who is set against the Lord of Israel and Judah.

The setting for the taunt is *sheol*, the place of the dead. The picture is a gathering of the great kings of the earth after the time of the earth receiving rest from the warfare that has been pronounced in 13:4*b*-8. The king of Babylon arrives in *sheol*, where he is met by the kings and leaders of the earth, who are amazed that even the mighty king of Babylon has met the same fate as they (vv. 9-11). They make a point of noting that in contrast to the wonderful conditions that that king had on earth his bed now is made up of maggots and his covering is of worms. That is highly figurative language noting the utter humiliation of the king of Babylon who stands for the anti-God forces that are against the people of God in Israel and Judah.

The portion of the oracle from verses 12-21 is a very controversial passage. Many interpreters see no one here except the king of Babylon. It has been pointed out that many of the expressions used of him in verses 12-14 were appellations of the Assyrian kings. Often, exaggerated and extravagant language was used in the records when the king was being described.

Other interpreters believe (as did some of the church fathers) that in this paragraph the king of Babylon is viewed as a tool or a front for the real, unseen ruler of the cosmos. They believe that God is addressing Satan, who is called in the New Testament the "prince of this world" (John 12:31; 14:30; 16:11 KJV; NASB has "ruler") and the "god of this age" (2 Cor. 4:4, literal translation).

There are a few other instances in Scripture in which Satan is addressed through one of his instruments. The earliest, of course, was in Eden after the Fall, when God addressed Satan through the serpent (Gen. 3:15), and in the New Testament the Lord Jesus said to Peter, "Get behind Me, Satan!" (Matt. 16:23). The passage under discussion could most closely be connected with Ezekiel 28:1-19, where many also believe that Satan is being addressed through the human king of Tyre.

In addressing this one God calls him "star of the morning" (NASB and NIV*). The KJV uses the equivalent Latin term *Lucifer*, which has become generally known in English as a title for Satan before his fall. The statement of the Lord Jesus in Luke 10:19 seems to be parallel to that. The Hebrew word simply means "bright one." A passage in the book of Job apparently refers to the angels as the "morning stars" (Job 38:7), although it uses different vocabulary. And in Revelation, Satan is seen as controlling a third part of the stars of heaven (Rev. 12:4).

The Lord Jesus is also called the "bright morning star" (Rev. 22:16). If this address in Isaiah is indeed to Satan, he is the false daystar in contrast to the Lord Jesus, the true One (2 Pet. 1:19, KJV).

This passage should be compared with Ezekiel 28:12-19, which seems to be a similar cryptic message to Satan. Ezekiel views the career of Satan from the beginning forward to its end, whereas Isaiah sees his career from its end backward to its beginning. Many Bible students consider Isaiah 14:12-17 to be the central passage in the Bible on the origin of sin. The fall from heaven mentioned in verse 12 is in reality a prophecy. The sin or moral fall described belongs to the dateless past, but the final expulsion of Satan from heaven evidently will not occur until the end time, at the middle of that period often spoken of as the seventieth week of Daniel (Dan. 9; Rev. 12:9).

One must be careful to hold to the teachings of the Bible and to avoid prevalent misconceptions arising from Milton's *Paradise Lost* and other literary works. The five "I wills" uttered by the "morning star" constitute the very essence of sin, culminating in the boast "I will make myself like the Most High" (14:14). If the human king of Babylon exalted himself as a god, certainly Satan

---

* *New International Version.*

has to the highest degree. Ezekiel describes the "anointed cherub" as being lifted up because of his beauty (Ezek. 28:14, 17), having been perfect or blameless in all his ways until iniquity was found in him (v. 15). Likewise, in the New Testament Paul warns against being lifted up with pride and falling into the very condemnation into which the devil fell (1 Tim. 3:6).

Isaiah summed up his message against Babylon in verses 24-27 by noting that the Lord had planned out all of those things and there was no one who could change the direction of the events of history. Assyria will be broken, and the Assyrians can do nothing to save themselves. It is interesting to note that that is exactly what the Assyrians were saying to Judah when Sennacherib was besieging Jerusalem.

THE ORACLE CONCERNING PHILISTIA (14:28-32)

In this oracle Isaiah tells of events in the area of Philistia, which was the coastal area along the Mediterranean Sea. He noted that "the rod that struck you is broken" (v. 29). The oracle is dated 715 B.C. (the death of Ahaz being mentioned in v. 28) and speaks of a temporary setback of Assyria that caused the Philistines to propose an alliance with Judah. Isaiah warned that the situation would not last and that further trouble would come (v. 29b). The Philistine region would be destroyed, whereas Israel was destined for the region of Palestine (vv. 31-32).

THE ORACLE CONCERNING MOAB (15:1—16:14)

The "burden of Moab" is a reminder of the origin of that nation from the incestuous relationship of Lot with one of his own daughters (Gen. 19:37). Moabites were excluded from the congregation of Israel to the tenth generation (Deut. 23:3). That obviously did not apply to women, because Ruth the Moabitess first married Mahlon, and after his death Boaz, thus coming into the line of the promised Redeemer (Ruth 4:10, 13, 22).

Under Uzziah, Moab had been a tributary state to Judah. This prophecy in its near view describes calamities coming on Moab resulting from the Assyrian invasions. Note that much of it comes "within three years" (16:14). The remnant of the Moabites fled to Edom in the face of the Assyrian invasion. Sela (16:1), the ancient capital of Edom, built among the rocky crags, is the city later known and still known as Petra, the city southeast of the Dead Sea in the present-day Jordan.

When the Moabites sought asylum in Judah, they were denied because of Moab's insolent arrogance (16:6). The passage should be compared with Ezekiel 25:8-11, another prophecy of judgment against Moab in Babylonian times.

Moab was one of the area states brought under subjection to Assyria. On several occasions that small nation-state was forced to pay tribute to Assyria, as is well attested in the Assyrian records. Isaiah begins the oracle by declaring that Moab will be completely destroyed (15:1-9). The lamentation is filled with place names. The extreme depression and humiliation of the people are noted in verse 2.

Isaiah then notes that a time will come when Judah will be the protector of Moab and Israel the means of protection and justice. That, of course, will be in the period of rest (the millennium), when the whole earth will look to Israel for peace and safety.

The reason for Moab's destruction is given in verses 6-12. Assyria is the means of the destruction, but the cause is the pride and arrogance of the nation of Moab (v. 6). Moab had thought it was strong and had at times set itself against Israel. God brought Moab to justice for that attitude of arrogance.

Isaiah gave a specific time structure for the destruction of Moab. It would have been an easy matter in Isaiah's day for the people of Jerusalem to determine whether or not the Lord was speaking through him by checking the prophetic word he was speaking. If Moab was destroyed as Isaiah was claiming, the people could have confidence in the rest of his prophetic words.

THE ORACLE CONCERNING DAMASCUS (17:1-14)

This oracle was apparently written while Damascus was still considered a buffer between the Assyrian Empire and Judah. Isaiah prophesied that there would be a time very soon when the dependence on Syria as a buffer would be useless, because Syria would be overrun. In verses 1-3 Isaiah describes the downfall of Syria (with Damascus as its capital). The culmination is that Damascus will be like Israel (v. 3b); that is, it will be utterly defeated.

Isaiah compares the destruction of Syria to the destruction in the end time judgment when the Lord will come to judge the peoples of the earth (vv. 4-11). It will be a time of sickliness and incurable pain, when people will look to the "Holy One of Israel" for help (v. 7) because He will be the only One who can save them from the situation in which they will find themselves.

The result of the judgment of the peoples will be like that of the fall of Damascus. The people will be blown away like chaff in the wind. There will be no help for them. Isaiah notes that this is the certain end of the peoples who pillage Judah (v. 14).

THE ORACLE CONCERNING THE LAND OF WHIRRING WINGS (18:1-7)

Chapter 18 is one of the most difficult chapters in the book to interpret. The "land of whirring wings" (v. 1) has been identified in various ways. Much nonsense has been written about the chapter, including the attempt to label it as a prophecy about the United States of America.

Undoubtedly the prophecy concerns Ethiopia (Cush), whose ruler, Tirhakah (2 Kings 19:9), conquered Egypt and resisted the Assyrian monarch Sennacherib. The Ethiopians were characterized as coming from the land of the tsetse fly, and thus the name of the prophecy.

Isaiah says two things about the people from this land. First, they will be defeated and the whole area will be open for the wild beasts to roam. Second, the people from this region will bring gifts to Israel during the millennial period. They will come to worship the Lord of hosts in Zion. Isaiah is painting a picture of a time when Israel will be the center of world affairs rather than a small struggling nation that is oppressed by Assyria.

THE ORACLE CONCERNING EGYPT (19:1—20:6)

Egypt had been traditionally seen as an enemy of Israel since the time of the sojourn of the Israelites there. This oracle contains the startling information that in the future Egypt will worship the Lord. Even more startling is the fact that Egypt and Assyria, bitter enemies in Isaiah's day, will worship together and have an alliance.

The oracle is divided into two parts. Chapter 19 contains the information about Egypt's future during the millennium. Chapter 20 contains Isaiah's prophecy that Egypt will soon be conquered by Assyria under Sargon.

ISAIAH TELLS OF EGYPT'S FUTURE (19:1-25)

Isaiah notes that Egypt will be beset by internal troubles (vv. 1-4). The Lord is said to be "riding on a swift cloud" (v. 1) to bring judgment on Egypt. The "cruel master" and the "mighty king" (v. 4) apparently refer to the Assyrian Empire and its ruler who will defeat them (cf. 20:1-6). Isaiah prophesied that the climate of Egypt will be drier than before and that the entire economy will suffer as a result (vv. 5-10). The wisest of the men of Egypt will be shown to be fools before God and His plan (vv. 11-15). The leaders of the nation and its wise men "have led Egypt astray" (v. 13) by not taking into consideration the Lord of Israel and His plans. Isaiah prophesies the time when Israel will control Egypt (vv. 16-17) and Egypt will swear allegiance to the Lord of Israel (v. 18). Worship of the one true God will be instituted in Egypt (vv. 19-22) and there will be peace on earth, even throughout the empires that were most warlike in Isaiah's day (vv. 23-25).

ISAIAH PROPHESIES ABOUT EGYPT'S FALL (20:1-6)

The normal poetic style of the oracles is broken with this short, almost parenthetical, narrative concerning the fall of Egypt and Ethiopia. Ethiopia's fortunes had been detailed in chapter 18. Egypt's future had been described in chapter 19. However, there apparently were still some in Judah who wanted to rely on the southern powers for protection against Assyria. Isaiah's sign of appearing as a captive person (v. 2) was given to show the nation it could not depend on the southern powers for safety from Assyria. God had already stated that He would cause Egypt to fall (19:1-4). The people should believe and depend on Him for their protection. The inhabitants of the coastlands will see the fall of Egypt and Ethiopia and realize that there is no future for them in alliances (v. 6).

THE ORACLE CONCERNING THE DESERT (21:1-10)

This is one of the more difficult oracles. In this section Isaiah prophesies a terrible event that is going to happen in the desert area around Israel where mobile populations flourished. He is terrified by the prospects of the situation. Often, because of the mention of Babylon in verse 9, the vision has been interpreted as referring to the fall of Babylon at the time of Cyrus. However, that event is always pictured as a time of joy for the nation of Israel, for it led to the liberation of the people of Judah. This event, on the contrary, is one that terrifies Isaiah. It is much more likely that he is giving a prophecy about the fall of Babylon to the Assyrians, perhaps in 689 B.C., which caused a feeling of despair among the other powers of the Near East as they realized there was going to be little they could do to stop the advance of the Assyrian Empire. Isaiah's picture of the terror and gloom also seems to represent the time of terror and fear that will be present at the end of the age.

THE ORACLE CONCERNING EDOM (21:11-12)

This short oracle concerns the area to the east of Israel. The question is put to the watchmen about the duration of the night—will it get better soon? The watchmen are not able to answer in the affirmative. They can give no hope that better times are ahead. Through this prophecy Isaiah apparently was countering the belief in the nation that good times were just around the corner.

THE ORACLE CONCERNING ARABIA (21:13-17)

This oracle depicts the effect of the political instability on the wandering tribes of Arabia. They are not able to count on even the necessities of life because of the warfare that is going on. Isaiah prophesied that the whole area would fall within a year (v. 16). Once again this specific prophecy would allow the people of Judah to see that he was speaking the truth and that God was speaking through him.

THE ORACLE CONCERNING THE VALLEY OF VISION (JERUSALEM) (22:1-25)

This oracle has several parts. First, Isaiah points out that the nation of Judah, centered at Jerusalem, will be judged like the other nations coming under the judgment of God (vv. 1-11). Isaiah is not specific as to what judgment he is speaking about here. Ultimately, the Babylonian captivity will be the time of the breaking down of the walls of the city. His prophecy says that the people of Jerusalem should not think they could get off lightly without God's judgment upon them. He "planned it long ago" (v. 11).

In the second part of the oracle Isaiah contrasts the present time of feasting and gladness with the time to come, which will be a time of sadness and humiliation (vv. 12-14). He states strongly that the judgment will come upon them—they cannot escape it (v. 14).

The third part of the oracle is concerned with two individuals who were apparently members of the royal court (vv. 15-25). The first, Shebna, is bitterly denounced by Isaiah (vv. 15-19). Isaiah prophesies that Shebna will be deposed from his important position in the court. Apparently, Shebna had much to do with the attitude Isaiah attacked in verses 12-14. In contrast to Shebna, Eliakim will be raised to a position of power within the court. Unlike Shebna, he will be a credit to his household. However, eventual destruction will come on the nation (v. 25).

THE ORACLE CONCERNING TYRE (23:1-18)

The final oracle concerns the destruction of Tyre, a city known as the greatest trade and commercial city of this era. Ezekiel 28 describes in great detail the splendor of Tyre's trading contracts. At the heart of Isaiah's oracle stands the world's worship of material things. When Tyre falls, the whole world weeps because the material system is being destroyed (vv. 1-7). Isaiah reveals that the destruction of the trading empire of Tyre was the Lord's doing (vv. 8-18). Because of the Assyrian conquest of Mesopotamia, the entire trading network was thrown into confusion. In verses 15-18 Isaiah prophesies of a time of seventy years in which Tyre will not be able to flourish in its business activities (about 700-630 B.C.). After that time Tyre again flourished as a leader in world trade.

CONCLUSION OF THE BURDENS

In these oracles or *burdens* Isaiah has shown what was to happen over the next several generations in the Near East as a result of the Assyrian march westward. His contemporaries would be able to judge his accuracy and determine whether or not God was speaking those words to them. Isaiah was warning the nation of Judah not to count on foreign alliances but rather to trust in the work of God on its behalf. The downfall of the nations was planned by God. There could be no deviation from His plan. Isaiah has also given an occasional glimpse of the situation in the last days, when the nations would once again be judged for their actions.

4

Punishment Followed by Kingdom Blessing

$(24:1 — 27:13)$

This section has been called by some commentators "Isaiah's little apocalypse." In apocalyptic prophecy the prophet is allowed by God to witness the future spread out as a panorama. Thus, he visually experiences what is coming to pass. Outstanding examples of apocalyptic prophecies in the Scriptures are found in Ezekiel, Daniel, Zechariah and, of course, in the Apocalypse, the book of Revelation.

Isaiah's repetition of themes has been noted several times, particularly the repetition of the two major themes of judgment and comfort. In chapters 24-27 the same sequence that is continually encountered in this book is seen again. It seems as though God would convince His people by sheer force of repetition. In fact, this is the order of life, and is found in other places as well as in Isaiah: first suffering, then glory. So it was with our blessed Lord Himself: "Seeking to know what person or time the Spirit of Christ within them was indicating as He predicted the sufferings of Christ and the glories to follow" (1 Pet. 1:11). It is the same with believers:

If indeed we suffer with Him in order that we may also be glorified with Him. [Rom. 8:17]

And after you have suffered for a little while, the God of all grace, who called you to His eternal glory in Christ, will Himself perfect, confirm, strengthen and establish you. [1 Pet. 5:10]

The outline of this section may be connected to that of the whole book in this way:

IV. Punishment Followed by Kingdom Blessing (24:1—27:13)
   A. Troubles Followed by the Reign of the Lord of Hosts
      (24:1-23)
   B. Praise of God for His Wonderful Works (25:1-12)
   C. A Song of Salvation (26:1-19)
   D. God's Indignation and the Regathering of Israel (26:20—
      27:13)

TROUBLES FOLLOWED BY THE REIGN OF THE LORD OF HOSTS
(24:1-23)

At the beginning of chapter 24 the prophecy turns away from
the burdens (God's grievous judgments on the Gentile nations) to
God's own people. The judgments that are coming on Judah will
be such as to empty the land (v. 3). The same Hebrew word can be
translated either "earth" or "land." Here it seems to refer to the
land of Israel rather than to the worldwide devastation pictured in
Revelation and other Scripture passages.

The immediate reference is undoubtedly to the Babylonian
conquests and the transmigration of the population according to
the custom of that day. All classes of the people will suffer. The
passage makes it clear that these judgments are retributive—that
God is taking vengeance for the sins of His people (v. 5). The
capture and desolation of Jerusalem is most emphatically included
in the judgment (v. 12). The prophet Jeremiah, who lived a
century after Isaiah's time and through the terrible period of
the Babylonian invasions, elaborates on some of those prophecies.

Even in the midst of grievous afflictions there will be those who
will glorify the Lord "in the fires" (v. 15, KJV). That is the
response of the godly remnant, so different from the general
populace, but always present in any era.

This is obviously a prophecy of the Babylonian conquest and
captivity, but that captivity manifestly does not exhaust its full
import, for the prophet looks ahead to "that day" (v. 21). The
catastrophic disruptions on earth and the signs in the heavenly
bodies seem to go far beyond the Babylonian desolations, terrible
as those were to be. There is undoubtedly a foreshadowing of
those cataclysmic judgments that are to overtake the "earth-
dwellers" in the end time, described so graphically in the book of
Revelation.

That this double fulfillment is in view seems to be conclusively shown by the allusion to the reign of the Lord of hosts on Mount Zion, in Jerusalem (v. 23). The glorious kingdom age will be a time of rejoicing and praise to God for the people of God, both the glorified saints of all ages (including the church) and the as yet unglorified subjects of the millennial kingdom, including living Israel of that day and a great multitude of Gentiles (Matt. 25:41).

PRAISE OF GOD FOR HIS WONDERFUL WORKS (25:1-12)

The contemplation of God's literally earthshaking works brings forth an exclamation of praise: "O LORD, Thou art my God; I will exalt Thee, I will give thanks to Thy name; for Thou hast worked wonders, plans formed long ago, with perfect faithfulness" (v. 1).

It is important to observe the harmony of the Old and New Testaments. In this chapter are found examples of Old Testament teachings that are carried over into the New Testament and amplified there. Verse 8 is referred to by Paul in 1 Corinthians 15:54 and the second clause of verse 8 is restated in Revelation 7:17 and 21:4.

In "that day" God's people will be glad they waited for Him (v. 9). That is indeed a contrast to the impatience of the restless world. Patient waiting is the difficult but sublime appointment for God's people. It will not always be so. The day of waiting, interminable though it sometimes seems, will have an end; the day of rejoicing in God's completed salvation will be eternal.

A SONG OF SALVATION (26:1-19)

The song of praise that begins chapter 26 will be sung "in that day"; that is, in the kingdom age when it will be completely appropriate. Now it cannot be sung in its full meaning. Thankfully, however, a timeless application can be made now or at any time. No matter in what period of history he lives, the believer can find in God the perfect peace described in the song (v. 3). Note that the Hebrew idiom is: "in peace, in peace," correctly rendered by the English translators as "in perfect peace" (KJV, NASB, NIV). It would be interesting to trace the many hymns and gospel songs that have been based on that passage. Frances Havergal's hymn "Like a River Glorious" not only draws on the verse indirectly in its first stanza, but goes on in its refrain to paraphrase the verse:

Stayed upon Jehovah hearts are fully blessed,
Finding as He promised, perfect peace and rest.

Perhaps best known of all is Augustus M. Toplady's immortal hymn "Rock of Ages" (written in 1776), with its title taken from the literal rendering of the Hebrew in verse 4: "For in Yahweh is the Rock of ages."

GOD'S INDIGNATION AND THE REGATHERING OF ISRAEL
(26:20—27:13)

The indignation mentioned in this passage (26:20) is the Day of the Lord, mentioned so many times in the Prophets. In that period of judgment the godly remnant of Israel will be protected (cf. Rev. 12:1-12). The church, raptured to meet the Lord Jesus (1 Thess. 4:16-18), will be *kept out of* the tribulation (cf. Rev. 3:10); the godly remnant of Israel will be *kept through* the tribulation.

The punishment of the inhabitants of the earth for their iniquity (v. 21) is described in considerable detail in the book of Revelation.

The mention of the vineyard in 27:2-6 portrays a different set of circumstances from the song of the vineyard in chapter 5. The prediction that Israel "will fill the whole world with fruit" (v. 6) is similar to Paul's exclamation in Romans about the blessing that will come on the world when Israel is restored:

Now if their transgression be riches for the world and their failure be riches for the Gentiles, how much more will their fulfillment be! . . . For if their rejection be the reconciliation of the world, what will their acceptance be but life from the dead? [Rom. 11:12, 15]

Chapter 27 closes with a description of the regathering of Israel, a gathering such as the world has not seen. This is undoubtedly the same regathering mentioned by the Lord Jesus Christ in Matthew 24:31:

And He will send forth His angels with *a great trumpet* and *they will gather together* His elect from the four winds, from one end of the sky to the other. [Italics added]

5

Pronouncement of Woes

$$(28:1 — 33:24)$$

As he carries out further the general theme of judgment, the prophet of God pronounces a series of "woes" on Israel and Judah particularly. It will be helpful to compare this series with other pronouncements of woe in other parts of Scripture. One such is the castigation of the Pharisees by the Lord Jesus Christ with its sevenfold "Woe to you, scribes and Pharisees, hypocrites!" (Matt. 23:13-15, 23, 25, 27, 29; cf. also v. 16).

Another is the series of terrifying woes in the end time, at the blowing of the fifth, sixth, and seventh trumpets in Revelation (Rev. 8:13).

Consider this outline:

V. Pronouncement of Woes (28:1—33:24)
    A. Woe to Ephraim (28:1-13)
    B. Warning to the Rulers of Judah (28:14-29)
    C. Woe to Jerusalem (Ariel) (29:1-24)
    D. Woe to the Egyptian Alliance (30:1—31:9)
    E. The Righteous King Who Will Deliver (32:1-20)
    F. Woe to Assyria (33:1-24).

WOE TO EPHRAIM (28:1-13)

The Northern Kingdom is addressed as Ephraim because of the dominance of that tribe over the other tribes in the kingdom during much of Israel's history.

This prophecy is addressed to the city of Samaria, which Omri had built and made the capital of the Northern Kingdom (1 Kings 16:24). The city was situated on a high hill overlooking a beautiful and fruitful valley. Other glimpses of it in the prophets show its splendor and luxury. Samaria was soon to be destroyed by the Assyrian invaders. The reference to the "drunkards of Ephraim" (v. 1) is similar to the charges made against Israel by other prophets, especially by Amos (Amos 6:1-14) and Hosea (Hos. 4:1-19). Those two prophets ministered directly to the Northern Kingdom. Amos's ministry was shortly before Isaiah's time and Hosea's overlapped with Isaiah's. Note also that Micah, although ministering primarily to Judah as Isaiah did, began his work with a reference to the fall of Samaria (Mic. 1:5-7).

The fulfillment of the woe on Ephraim was not long in coming. Even as Isaiah spoke, Ephraim's flower was fading (v. 1). Assyria was about to conquer and destroy the Northern Kingdom.

The Bible frequently stresses the evil of drunkenness (Prov. 20:1; 23:29-35). It views it not as a weakness to be pitied but as a sin to be condemned. The sin was particularly heinous because it was the sin of those in places of leadership who needed clear heads for governing.

It is important to be alert to the interweaving of events in the prophet's day and the allusions to future messianic times. The expression *in that day* (v. 5) seems to indicate its complete fulfillment in the time when Christ will be reigning. The reference to the Lord as a "glorious diadem to the remnant of His people" appears also to look forward to the future deliverance and blessing.

Priests and prophets (v. 7), who are especially supposed to give people help from God, were unable to help because they, too, were engulfed in the universal sin of drunkenness (v. 7). This is a very sad description of the conditions of the time.

The people resented bitterly the prophet's admonitions to them and mocked his methods. They felt that he was treating them like children (vv. 9-10). "Very well," he replied, "God will have to instruct you through men who speak a different language— obviously through the Assyrian invaders" (v. 11).

WARNING TO THE RULERS OF JUDAH (28:14-29)

The prophecy has now shifted from Samaria to the Southern Kingdom, as is clear from verse 14. This paragraph presumably condemns the Egyptian alliance although some commentators take it to refer to the pro-Assyrian party. Whatever the details, there were parties and factions in Judah favorable to each of the dominant powers of the day—the ferocious Assyrians and the somewhat waning Egyptians.

Just as in a former section God promised hope through the coming Immanuel (chapters 7-12), so here He gives assurance of ultimate deliverance through the One who is the "costly cornerstone" (v. 16). Some deny that there could be any kind of messianic reference in this context, but other teachings concerning the Lord Jesus Christ as a "stone" fit in with that. This passage is parallel also to the prophecy of Immanuel, for it looks far ahead. Time is not a problem with God, and His Book is for His people of all times and periods. How refreshing it is in the midst of warnings of doom to be able to see the promised Redeemer! This is the same "stone" mentioned by the psalmist when he said, "The stone which the builders rejected has become the chief corner stone" (Ps. 118:22). That Psalm 118:22 is clearly messianic is attested by the apostle Peter (1 Pet. 2:6) and the apostle Paul (Eph. 2:20-22). The sneering unbelief of the rulers is detestable. Those in places of leadership in Judah who should have learned from the tragic example of Israel smugly relied on their unholy treaties of alliance, disregarding the promises and warnings of God.

In contrast to their refuge of lies (v. 15), God affirms that He will set up a sure foundation (v. 16; cf. 1 Cor. 3:11).

This is one of the glories of Isaiah, that he constantly turns one's thoughts toward Christ, who is our Immanuel (7:14), our Prince of Peace (9:6), our Rock of Ages (26:4), our chief Cornerstone (28:16). There is no ground for attaching this statement to anyone of Isaiah's day, even if one were to make such a person a type or foreshadowing of Christ. Such passages as this attest the divine origin and unity of the Scriptures.

The Lord Jesus Christ is for the believing remnant of Israel the "precious cornerstone" (KJV), as He is also for the church (Eph. 2:20). But for unbelieving Israel He is "a stone of stumbling" and "a rock of offense" (Isa. 8:14, KJV; cf. Rom. 9:33). For the Gentile nations He will be the smiting stone (Dan. 2:32, 35, 45). For the believer of any dispensation He is "the shadow of a great rock in a weary land" (Isa. 32:2, KJV).

WOE TO JERUSALEM (ARIEL) (29:1-24)

Jerusalem is now addressed under the poetic name *Ariel* (v. 1). Most Hebrew scholars seem to believe that *Ariel* means "lion of God," although some render it "hearth of God," and connect it with what is said in verse 2 about an "altar hearth" (NIV). The meaning "lion of God" would refer to the many blessings and glories of the city through the centuries.

Here again there seems to be a blending of events near at hand with those in the distant future. The near event was the invasion by the Assyrians under Sennacherib. The distant event is the invasion of the land of Israel by a coalition of armies in the end time under the beast (Antichrist) shortly before the coming of Christ in glory and the setting up of the millennial kingdom.

The judgment is because of hypocrisy on the part of those who were enjoying privileges as the people of God. They were addicted, as has already been seen in chapter 1, to a formalistic religion that did not touch the heart (v. 13). As always in the prophecies the judgment is not total, for there is a glimpse of future restoration and glory (vv. 17-24). Jennings's comment on this section (originally we said *apposite*, not opposite) is appropriate and helpful.

> The oppressor and the scoffer have long been in the ascendancy; in that day of which our prophet speaks, they will be looked for in vain. But again, mark the divine hatred and repulsion of all Pharisaic claims to superior holiness.
>
> Happy picture of Israel's future, and well, indeed, for us if we can personally appropriate its precious lesson, and trust our God who weaves our web of time with intermingling of mercy and of judgment.[1]

WOE TO THE EGYPTIAN ALLIANCE (30:1—31:9)

One of the solemn warnings God had given through Moses to the people of Israel and to their future kings was that they were not to depend on Egypt (Deut. 17:16). They were not to go to Egypt to multiply horses, silver and gold, or wives. Throughout Israel's history many kings had broken that commandment. Even Solomon, in spite of all his greatness, was exceedingly guilty.

Through Isaiah, God warned the people that their dependence on Egypt would not help them. In Judah in the days of Ahaz, when the powerful Assyrian Empire threatened, it was the natural tendency to turn to the only world power that seemed capable of

1. F. C. Jennings, *Studies in Isaiah*, p. 355.

standing up to Assyria—Egypt. One of the hardest lessons that we as people of God need to learn is that of total dependence on Him (cf. John 15:5).

Warning that Egypt cannot help, God chides His people with their lack of trust in Himself. The people of Judah are addressed as "rebellious children" (30:1), a title reminiscent of the opening of the book (1:2).

How often such a scene has been repeated in the history of God's people! The conflict between reason and faith is often a bitter one, chiefly because the *reason* is that of expediency, and the *faith* seems so remote. But such reasoning is not actually reasonable, because it leaves out the one all-important factor, the Person of God. The old saying "One with God is a majority" remains true but is seldom heeded. The false prophets who advised an Egyptian alliance were heeded partly because they advocated action in a terrible emergency. The impatience of the human heart was not satisfied by the admonition of the true prophet of God: "For thus the Lord GOD, the Holy One of Israel has said, 'In repentance and rest you will be saved, in quietness and trust is your strength. But you were not willing'" (v. 15).

That is not a mere quietism or passivism that is enjoined. It is a returning *to God*; a rest *in God*. It is not a reliance on quietness, but a reliance on Him who can give quietness to the restless soul of man. That is in contrast to a peculiar philosophy of the world that is often heard: "Just have faith and everything will be all right." Faith in what? Or more to the point, faith in whom? God is the answer to all problems and the only answer.

"But you were not willing" (v. 15). Centuries later the Lord Jesus Christ in His lament over Jerusalem uttered practically those same words (Matt. 23:37). Human beings are prone to blame God for their troubles when they themselves are the cause. But man's rebellion, no matter how reprehensible, cannot forever keep God from manifesting His grace. God promised to those people, undeserving as they were, deliverance from the Assyrians (30:31). When the deliverance came it occurred in such a way that all could see it was the Lord's doing.

Chapter 31 begins with a summation of why God's judgment is coming on His people. They are relying on Egypt, not on Him. The Egyptians are men and not God (v. 3). God is seen as waging war on Mount Zion (v. 4). God's deliverance from Assyria in the prophet's day (Isa. 37:35-36) is again seen as a foreshadowing of the even greater deliverance from Antichrist in the end time. Unless one sees the swinging of the pendulum back and forth from the near view to the far view, much that is in the prophecy is incomprehensible.

THE RIGHTEOUS KING WHO WILL DELIVER (32:1-20)

Here is the answer to the world's unrest: "A king will reign righteously" (v. 1). Kings have reigned with varying degrees of ability and success, but there has never been any king like that. Many commentators take this verse to be a reference to Hezekiah who, of course, was righteous compared to his father Ahaz. Although one would not want to detract at all from Hezekiah's remarkable career as one of the great reforming kings of Judah, this prophecy is clearly an allusion to messianic times. The One seen here is the Lord Jesus Christ Himself. He is perfectly righteous and can reign in righteousness. Many who would like to have world peace do not want it to come in this way. "And the work of righteousness will be peace" (v. 17). When a king reigns in righteousness, unrighteous people may well tremble in fear.

The description of the righteous King, coming as it does amidst the solemn pronouncement of woes, gives hope to the godly remnant. Righteousness will characterize this future kingdom of Messiah. Because righteousness will be enforced and a true sense of values will be substituted for a false sense, there will be a wonderful revolution in the social and political orders. "No longer will the fool be called noble, or the rogue be spoken of as generous" (v. 5).

When one thinks of the misguided and hypocritical "bowing and scraping" before so many evil and undeserving rulers in the satanic world-system, one can be greatly encouraged that such demagoguery and sycophancy are not going to continue forever. The hope of a righteous ruler to come is compared to "a shelter from the storm" and likened to "the shade of a huge rock in a parched land" (v. 2).

The recognition of the glories of the future helps to prepare God's people to withstand the stormy present. Often in the prophecies the far view (at least that which New Testament readers now recognize as the far view) mingles with the near view. That at times can be perplexing, but Peter informs us that even the prophets themselves were perplexed with such matters (1 Pet. 1:10-12).

The warning to the complacent women, beginning at verse 9, is evidently referring to the imminent Assyrian invasion, but then the prophecy looks again toward messianic times:

Until the Spirit is poured out upon us from on high, and the wilderness becomes a fertile field. . . . Then justice will dwell in the wilderness, and righteousness will abide in the fertile field. [vv. 15-16]

WOE TO ASSYRIA (33:1-24)

A distinction is drawn between the nation as a whole and the godly remnant. It is the remnant that speaks in verse 2: "O *Lord*, be gracious to us; we have waited for Thee. Be Thou their strength every morning, our salvation also in the time of distress."

While the book of Isaiah is filled with figures of speech and poetic language in general, one must not suppose that they represent a visionary world of unreality. Rather, they point to a real situation. Someday such words as these will be literally true: "The *Lord* is exalted, for He dwells on high; He has filled Zion with justice and righteousness."

So much of the confusion in the interpretation of Isaiah and other Old Testament prophetic books comes from a refusal to distinguish between Israel and the church, which denies any future to Israel as a nation and equates the throne of David with God's throne in heaven. It is interesting that Christians who are eager to claim Israel's future blessings in the kingdom age are not at all willing to accept Israel's curses and judgments. Throughout Isaiah we see a reference to a future King. Invariably He is said to be the Fulfiller of the Davidic covenant and the One who will sit forever on David's throne, which is a historical entity.

To find the fulfillment of the numerous kingdom prophecies of the Old Testament in the present spiritual blessings of the church is to lose the literal thread of prophecy and to be without reference points. The only consistent hermeneutic is that which takes seriously and literally the numerous and sometimes extended Old Testament passages that speak of Israel's eternal possession of the land and the Davidic dynasty's eternal occupancy of the throne. In fact, the New Testament opens in that way, showing that Jesus Christ is the fulfiller of both the Abrahamic and the Davidic covenants (Matt. 1:1).

When one follows a literal interpretation that allows the recognition of dispensational distinctions, one can come to a satisfactory conclusion.

Isaiah 32 is found to be in perfect harmony with 7:14; 9:6-7; 11:1, and other passages in Isaiah and the Old Testament. Psalm 2 is a central passage that sets the tone for the future kingdom of the Messiah. One who sees Psalm 2 as a missionary message for the present day is in a hopeless morass.

Chapter 33 pronounces woe on the "destroyer" (v. 1), the Assyrian ruler Sennacherib. The miraculous deliverance brought by the Lord after the blasphemous statements of Sennacherib and his chief spokesmen is described in the historical section, chapters 36 and 37 (cf. also 2 Kings 18-19).

Since Assyria was the great enemy of God's people in Isaiah's time, victory over that power was a foreshadowing of Christ's future worldwide dominion over the nations. There is a constant recognition in the prophecies that deliverance comes through the direct intervention of God (see v. 22).

6

Indignation and Glory

$(34:1 — 35:10)$

After the section on the woes, Isaiah calls on all nations to hear another summation of God's purposes:

> Draw near, O nations, to hear; and listen,
>   O peoples!
> Let the earth and all it contains hear, and the
>   world and all that springs from it.
> For the LORD's indignation is against all the
>   nations,
> And His wrath against all their armies;
>   He has utterly destroyed them,
> He has given them over to slaughter.
>
> [34:1-2]

A suggested outline of chapters 34 and 35 is:

VI. Indignation and Glory (34:1—35:10)
    A. The Lord's Indignation (34:1-17)
    B. The Blossoming Desert (35:1-10)

THE LORD'S INDIGNATION (34:1-17)

Some people refuse to believe that God manifests anger. They think that His love is an easy-going toleration of anything and everything, a universal condoning of human behavior. However, the Scriptures frequently speak of the wrath of God and show that there will be a time when His righteousness will be vindicated through His judgment of the world.

His indignation is not the vengeful, selfish anger of sinful human beings, but rather the holy wrath of outraged majesty. God would not be God if He allowed evil to go on forever unpunished and unchecked. As the prophet says, this indignation of the Lord is directed against nations universally (v. 2). It is not limited to Isaiah's time or to the coming destruction of the Assyrian army. It is the end-time judgment on all nations, the outpouring of God's wrath on the whole world. As the psalmist says, "Then shall he speak unto them in his wrath, and vex them in his sore displeasure" (Ps. 2:5, KJV). That looks forward unmistakably to the time when the Lord Jesus Christ will return to take over the government of the earth.

The day of the Lord's vengeance (v. 8) is graphically described in other passages of Scripture, both in the Old Testament (Joel, Zephaniah, Jeremiah, Ezekiel, Daniel, and Zechariah) and in the New (2 Thessalonians and supremely in the book of Revelation). In Revelation, the extended mention of the series of judgments included in the seven seals, the seven trumpets, and the seven bowls presents an awe-inspiring foreview of what God is going to do when He intervenes in human affairs. The earth-dwellers—those whose horizon is limited to this world—will then experience the indignation of God.

The truly believing heart can rest in the knowledge that things are going to be different from what they are now. Wrongs are to be righted, evil recompensed, and good rewarded. It was important for the people of Israel to know that as they faced the immediate future, which was bleak with the thought of judgment for the nation's sins. As they contemplated the terrible iniquity of the pagan nations around them, some of which (Assyria and Babylon) were the instruments of God's judgment on Israel and Judah (see Hab. 1:5-11), they did not need to question God or rail at Him in unbelief. Those nations and all nations ultimately will receive the due reward of their deeds. Thus the doctrine of the wrath of God, while fearsome to those who insist on being His enemies, is seen as the necessary and satisfying corollary to His love and grace.

In the face of passages such as this one, it is strange indeed that some people (even many scholars) can speak of the provincialism of the Old Testament as if the people of Israel thought of the Lord (Yahweh) only as a tribal or national God who had no concern for other people and nations. One of the dominant notes in Isaiah, as has been indicated from time to time, is *universality*. All nations are constantly in view. The salvation that is offered is worldwide in its applications as is the judgment that is to come. "The Lord's indignation is against all nations" (v. 2).

THE BLOSSOMING DESERT (35:1-10)

Just as the indignation of chapter 34 is universal, so also the glory of chapter 35 is universal. This chapter is a lovely poetic description of the condition of nature in the millennial kingdom. Its conditions will be accompaniments to the reign of Messiah.

Since the modern resettlement of the land by Jews from all over the world, and especially since the establishment of the state of Israel in 1948, the settlers have done wonders in restoring the fertility of the soil through scientific irrigation and cultivation. The *arabah* and the *negev* have indeed been cultivated beyond anything known in recent times. But that is certainly far short of the description in this chapter. The miracle of healing that the Lord Jesus Christ performed during His earthly ministry were a credential of His messiahship and a foreshadowing of the marvelous conditions that will characterize the millennium. Here nature is pictured as reflecting the glories that are to come to God's people. The New Testament asserts that the "whole creation groans and suffers the pains of childbirth together until now" (Rom. 8:22). Isaiah 35 is a prophecy of the time when the groaning will be over and the physical earth will be "set free from its slavery to corruption into the freedom of the glory of the children of God" (Rom. 8:21).

This chapter furnishes another illustration of Isaiah's use of constantly recurring themes. Here the "highway" is mentioned prominently again:

> And a highway will be there, a roadway,
> And it will be called the Highway of Holiness.
> The unclean will not travel on it,
> But it will be for him who walks that way,
> And fools will not wander on it.
>
> [v. 8]

It is prepared for God's elect, who will come back to their land from all parts of the earth. This concept of the highway is one of the many evidences of the unity of Isaiah (cf. 11:16 and 40:3). At the end of chapter 35 the "ransomed of the LORD" (v. 10) are seen returning to Zion with inexpressible joy. The same idea is repeated in Isaiah 51:11. It is strange that many of those who acknowledge the historicity of the Exodus, having no difficulty accepting the literalness of the narrative about Israel's coming out of Egypt and possessing the land of Canaan, seem to think that there is something crass or demeaning about taking such prophetic passages as this one literally. There is going to be a future day in which Israel will be regathered from all the earth as described here and in numerous other prophetic passages. The church in the New Testament has sufficient glories without appropriating Israel's blessings. This passage, along with many others, shows what God is going to do with this material planet when He removes the curse put on the physical creation as a result of Adam's sin. If the earth is so beautiful now, even though under a curse, what will it be like when the curse is removed! Passages such as this help to give us a foregleam of the wonders to come.

The acceptance of millennial glory does not detract in any way from the perfection of the eternal state. Both the millennium and the eternal state are in view in prophecy (cf. Isa. 65:17), but the emphasis in the Old Testament prophetical books seems to be on the millennial kingdom. God's theocratic purpose is in harmony with His redemptive purpose because His original mandate to Adam to rule the earth is ultimately going to be carried out fully by the Last Adam, who is the "Lord from heaven" (1 Cor. 15:47, KJV). The Redeemer, Jesus Christ, is also the "King of kings, and Lord of Lords" (Rev. 19:16).

7
Historical Interlude

$(36:1 - 39:8)$

Some commentators regard chapters 36-39 as a full-fledged division of the book, making the outline in three parts rather than two. However, it seems more convenient to consider this section as an integral part of the first main division. At any rate, many interpreters have agreed that these chapters form a bridge between the earlier chapters that deal with Assyria and the later chapters that anticipate the Babylonian period of world-domination and the coming Babylonian captivity. Isaiah lived, of course, in the Assyrian period, but his message had to do in large measure with the Babylonian captivity. (These chapters should be compared with 2 Kings 18-20 and 2 Chronicles 29-32. Second Kings 19 and Isaiah 37 are identical.)

The study of the Bible is not without its problems. One of those, in this particular context, concerns the dates of Hezekiah's reign. A related difficulty has to do with the two main events described in the section. What is the chronological relationship between the deliverance from Sennacherib's invasion and King Hezekiah's illness and miraculous recovery?

Edward J. Young has discussed these matters thoroughly in his commentary on Isaiah. The possibility he favors is that the text of Isaiah 36:1 should read "the twenty-fourth year of King Hezekiah" instead of "the fourteenth year." However, there is no manuscript evidence for such a reading. Most are agreed that the date of Sennacherib's withdrawal was 701 B.C. One of the serious problems arises from the other biblical statement that Hezekiah was already reigning when the Northern Kingdom was taken into

97

captivity by the Assyrians under Tiglath-pileser in 722 or 721 B.C. (2 Kings 18:1).

The conjecture that Hezekiah may have reigned jointly for a time with his father, Ahaz, and that the fourteenth year mentioned in Isaiah 36:1 refers to his sole reign has much in its favor. It would not be out of harmony with other similar situations in the history of both Israel and Judah. The student who wishes to pursue the complex subject of the chronology of Israel and Judah would do well to consult Thiele's study.[1]

If that is a true reconstruction of the time, then Hezekiah's illness and recovery, although described after the troubles with Sennacherib, would have taken place prior to those troubles, since the king was granted fifteen more years of life. The expression "in those days" in 38:1 would fit with this view. Young and others conjecture that the topics are arranged to heighten the "bridge" effect of the chapters. The first event—the Assyrian invasion and withdrawal—looks back to the earlier chapters of Isaiah that had to do with the Assyrian period; and the second event—Hezekiah's illness and recovery—points forward to the future Babylonian period through the visit of the Babylonian envoys to congratulate Hezekiah on his recovery.

The believing student should not hide his head in the sand about difficulties in the interpretation and understanding of Scripture. It must always be remembered that God has purposely designed His Word so that the element of faith must always be present. The casual or skeptical reader may often be stopped by the difficulties and seeming discrepancies. True faith will acknowledge the difficulties but will also understand that they can be resolved. Every solution that has come through the tireless efforts of many servants of God as they have pored over the Scriptures has caused the Scriptures to shine more resplendently. The Bible is a self-authenticating Book, and its central figure, the Lord Jesus Christ, is both self-authenticating and Bible-authenticating. His word that "the Scripture cannot be broken" (John 10:35) is a wonderful assurance.

Consequently, the proper procedure is to take the Scriptures at face value, compare Scripture with Scripture, study the background as much as we can, and wait on the Lord for the rest.

---

1. Edwin R. Thiele, *The Mysterious Numbers of the Hebrew Kings.* For a different point of view see Martin Anstey, *The Romance of Bible Chronology.*

If the invasion could be proved to be earlier than 701 B.C. there would be a possibility that the events in chapters 36-39 are recorded in chronological order. This whole question will have to be considered as unresolved at present.

GOD'S DELIVERANCE OF JERUSALEM FROM SENNACHERIB (36:1—37:38)

As seen previously, 36:1 contains one of the few dates in the book of Isaiah. Some years before that Assyria had swallowed up the Northern Kingdom. In subsequent years the Assyrian monarchs evidently considered Judah an easy prey. When one realizes that the city of Jerusalem was only about ten miles from the border between Israel and Judah, one can see how simple it was for the Assyrian ruler to deploy his forces against it. One can imagine the alarm in the city as word came of one walled town after another falling to the Assyrian invaders.

A delegation came from Sennacherib (v. 2) who was occupied with the siege of Lachish in the southwestern region of the kingdom of Judah. "Rabshakeh" is not a proper name, but a title of one of the leading Assyrian officials. The meeting between this scornful enemy and the emissaries took place in a location with historic associations, the same place where the prophet had gone out to meet King Ahaz with the prophecy of Immanuel (7:1). Sennacherib's own annals tell how he had shut up Hezekiah in Jerusalem "like a bird in a cage."

The tone of the rabshakeh was arrogant and scornful, correctly echoing the attitude of his master. It should be remembered that it was Hezekiah's father, Ahaz, who had gone against the word of the Lord through Isaiah in seeking Assyria's help and making an Assyrian alliance. As a part of his reforms, Hezekiah had been trying to break away from the Assyrian alliance, although even he made the mistake of relying on Egypt for help.

In reading the account one can sense the scorn of the rabshakeh by the fact that he did not even speak courteously to Hezekiah's envoys; that is, he simply used the king's name without using his title, King of Judah. One thing the Assyrian official said was true—that Egypt could not be relied on for safety (v. 6). He said Egypt was a broken reed and events proved that to be true. The rabshakeh berated the Judaic emissaries and actually claimed to be representing Yahweh in coming against Judah (v. 10). He evidently misunderstood or misrepresented what King Hezekiah had done in closing down the high places, alleging that such an action was against the Lord, while on the contrary it was just the opposite. Although speaking to the representatives of King Hezekiah, the rabshakeh was apparently talking loudly so he would be heard by those people of Jerusalem who were observing from the city wall. He was speaking in the Hebrew language and could therefore be understood by the assembled people. The Judaic envoys requested that he speak Aramaic, which in the eighth century had already become a sort of trade language or *lingua franca*, so as not to stir up the people.

Instead of acceding to their request, he returned coarse and insulting remarks in the people's own language, seeking to awaken in them terror and revulsion, by threatening them with a horrible famine that would ensue if they tried to withstand the Assyrian power.

That which doomed the Assyrians to failure was their blasphemous comparison of the true God with the "gods" of the nations, which understandably had not been able to deliver their devotees from the Assyrian king. Hezekiah's representatives returned to him with their clothes torn—the normal and authentic sign of mourning (v. 22). They had obeyed Hezekiah by not returning an answer to the taunts of the rabshakeh (v. 21). King Hezekiah knew what to do. He entered the house of the Lord and then sent for a word from the prophet Isaiah. The prophet replied by sending back a message of reassurance that God would deliver him from the arrogant king and his army. An interval elapsed during which the rabshakeh reported back to Sennacherib, who had been besieging Libnah (v. 8). There is some question as to whether the second message to Hezekiah was only a short time after the first, during the same campaign, or whether it came during a subsequent invasion of Judah. The former seems more likely.

This time Hezekiah received a menacing letter from Sennacherib, reiterating what had been said previously by the rabshakeh. Sennacherib noted that the Egyptians were on the march, under Tirhakah of the Cushite (Ethiopian) dynasty, and warned Hezekiah not to depend on them. Hezekiah, a truly godly man, spread out this letter before the Lord (37:14); not that he thought God needed to see it, but as an act of supplication, acknowledging that his help could only come from the Lord.

As mentioned previously, the Assyrian monarch blasphemously

equated Hezekiah's God with the gods of the nations he had conquered. Where were their gods when they needed them, he asked, and where were the kings of those nations now?

The prayer of Hezekiah (vv. 15-20) is an eloquent answer to those who allege that the Old Testament teaches a polytheistic or henotheistic religion. It is sometimes said by destructive critics of the Bible that the Hebrews in Old Testament times thought of the Lord as one among many gods, although He was their particular God. Such a view is a travesty on the Old Testament. Hezekiah believed in and expressed as clear an ethical monotheism as anyone possibly could. He knew that the so-called gods of the nations were nonentities and proclaimed it as clearly as the apostle Paul does in the New Testament (cf. v. 19 with 1 Cor. 8:4-6).

No doubt many in Isaiah's time doubted or wondered at the prophecy that God gave through Isaiah in answer to Hezekiah's prayer. Certainly from a human point of view the Assyrian army seemed more than capable of conquering the city of Jerusalem. But Sennacherib and his people did not know God; they had left Him out of their calculations, as unsaved people always do (Ps. 14:1). It was He who defended the city (v. 35).

The chapter closes with a very brief statement concerning the destruction in the Assyrian army brought about by the Angel of Yahweh (v. 36) and Sennacherib's departure and later murder in Nineveh by two of his sons. Secular historians have to admit that the Assyrians withdrew because of widespread disaster. Pestilence is the term most often used, but the context makes it clear that it was no ordinary pestilence. It was a direct judgment from God. The expression "the angel of Yahweh" is a term normally, though not always, used in the Old Testament to express a theophany (a manifestation of God). In these cases the "Messenger of Yahweh" is God Himself. The New Testament reveals Him to be the second Person of the Godhead (John 1:18).

HEZEKIAH'S ILLNESS AND MIRACULOUS RECOVERY (38:1—39:8)

The second major event in the historical interlude is the account of Hezekiah's critical illness and his miraculous healing. This event possibly occurred before Sennacherib's invasion previously described. The expression "in those days" (38:1) is fitting in this case. To answer the question why the prophet would place the two great events out of chronological order, it can be said that the Assyrian invasion was related to much that had preceded in the book, since the whole first half has much to say about Assyria and its relationship to the kingdom of Judah. It is as though the prophet is rounding out the Assyrian times by recording this major invasion and divine deliverance.

King Hezekiah's illness and recovery gives occasion to the narrative of the Babylonian envoys and links the prophet's time with the future Babylonian captivity, which loomed on the horizon and had such a prominent place in the prophetic message of Isaiah. That is what is meant by the "bridge effect" of this section.

There are other instances in Scripture of events being given out of chronological order when the purpose is to treat a series of happenings topically rather than chronologically. An instance is the three parts of the temptation of the Lord Jesus (cf. Matt. 4:1-11 with Luke 4:1-13).

From the statement of Scripture that Manasseh was twelve years old when Hezekiah died it appears that Hezekiah had no heir at the time Isaiah spoke to him about his impending death. That would account for the king's overwhelming sorrow. He turned his face to the wall (v. 2), not to pout like a child at the prophet's message but to close out all other influences while he communed with God about this dreadful news. God had promised that Israel would never be without a man to sit on David's throne (see the Davidic Covenant in 2 Sam. 7:4-17). Could God go back on His promise?

Some have raised the objection that God was trifling with Hezekiah by telling him he was going to die when God knew that He was going to spare him for fifteen more years. That is a problem with those who fail to see the parallel teachings in Scripture of God's sovereignty and man's responsibility. There are some things that God does absolutely without any secondary causes. There are other things that He chooses to do mediately through secondary causes of various kinds. And some things God has decreed that He will do only in answer to believing prayer. Hezekiah must exercise faith, look to God, and acknowledge that he had no hope apart from God's direct intervention. God's answer through the prophet in which He alludes to "your father David" (v. 5) is a reminder of the Davidic Covenant as an unconditional and unfailing determination on God's part.

The mention of deliverance from the king of Assyria in connection with Hezekiah's healing gives further credence to the view that the illness came before Sennacherib's invasion (v. 6).

There is some uncertainty about the precise nature of the sign God gave to Hezekiah. Whether the instrument referred to was an actual sundial or simply that time was reckoned as the shadow descended on a particular stairway is a matter of conjecture. Some affirm that true sundials were unknown in Judah at that time, but others with some evidence assert that the sundial was invented by the Babylonians in that century and that obviously Judah had some contact with the Babylonians even then, as evidenced by the coming of the envoys from Merodach-baladan (39:1). At any rate, what God did was a miracle, perhaps not as generally noticeable as the long day of Joshua (Josh. 10:13-14) but just as real and just as remarkable.

Isaiah 38 contains a very beautiful psalm written by King Hezekiah after his miraculous recovery (vv. 9-20). It is a striking testimony to the faith of this outstanding man. He recognized that salvation was even more important than the recovery of his physical health:

> Lo, for my own welfare I had great bitterness;
> It is Thou who hast kept my soul from the pit of nothingness,
> For Thou hast cast all my sins behind Thy back.
>
> [v. 17]

That prayer in the poetic form of a psalm can be compared to Jonah's similar prayer from the stomach of the great sea creature (Jonah 2:1-9). In each case the person involved came to realize his complete dependence on the Lord and cast himself wholly on Him. Yet, even godly men can make serious mistakes. Hezekiah, for all his faith and prayerfulness, seems to have given way to pride in showing all his wealth and that of the Temple to the delegation from Merodach-baladan, the Babylonian king. In another passage God tells us that the incident of the Babylonian envoys was permitted by God as a test of Hezekiah (2 Chron. 32:31). In that test he did not come out so admirably. Each of us can learn the lesson of our need for constant trust and dependence on God.

Victory in one battle does not automatically insure victory in the next. "Therefore let him who thinks he stands take heed lest he fall" (1 Cor. 10:12).

This event shows the historical background of the later Babylonian captivity, which is such an important topic in Isaiah's prophecy, especially in the second part of the book of Isaiah.

8

Deliverance of God's People

(40:1—48:22)

Mention has already been made of the general theme and arrangement of the second part of Isaiah. It looks through and beyond the Babylonian captivity that was announced by Isaiah to King Hezekiah at the close of chapter 39.

The general theme of the division is expressed in the opening verse of chapter 40: " 'Comfort, O comfort My people,' says your God" (40:1).

In this section the prophet is allowed to assume an ideal viewpoint and to see the Babylonian captivity as already past, although it did not even begin until long after his own time. As seen earlier, this part of the book is divided into three sections of nine chapters each. The sections are clearly marked off by the refrain of "No peace for the wicked" (48:22; 57:21). It fits into the basic outline in this way:

PART TWO: THE COMFORT OF GOD (40:1—66:24)
I. Deliverance of God's People (40:1—48:22)
II. The Suffering Servant as the Redeemer (49:1—57:21)
III. The Glorious Consummation (58:1—66:24).

Each of those sections is arranged symmetrically. The present chapter divisions apparently follow rather closely (with some exceptions) the logical divisions of the prophet's message (as noted earlier from Delitzsch, who referred to Rückert).

In the first nine chapters (40-48) the thought centers on the deliverance from Babylon, which is to be brought about by Cyrus, the Persian king. Cyrus is mentioned by name in the very heart of the section (44:28; 45:1). Throughout the section a contrast is drawn between Israel and the nations and Yahweh and the false gods. God's almighty power is demonstrated in contrast to the powerlessness of the idols. Above and beyond the deliverance of Israel from Babylon is the recognition of the greater deliverance through the Messiah, the Lord Jesus Christ.

The first section of the second part of the book can be outlined as follows:

I. Deliverance of God's People (40:1—48:22)
   A. The Comfort of God (40:1-31)
   B. Further Proof of the Lord's Power and Deity (41:1-29)
   C. The Lord's Servant Who Will Bring Judgment (42:1-25)
   D. Israel's Privilege and Responsibility as God's Servant (43:1-28)
   E. The Powerful God and the Powerless Idols (44:1-28)
   F. God's Purposes Through Cyrus, His Anointed (45:1-25)
   G. Judgment on Babylon's Idols (46:1-13)
   H. Judgment on the Babylonian Empire (47:1-15)
   I. Exhortations to the Impenitent and Unbelieving (48:1-22)

THE COMFORT OF GOD FOR DELIVERED ISRAEL (40:1-11)

The opening of chapter 40 strikes the keynote for all that follows in the book, just as 1:2 strikes the keynote for the first part. In both cases God speaks of Israel as "My people." What God purposes to do for His people He calls on men also to do. Some commentators believe that the command is addressed to the prophets as a group, but perhaps it is broader than that, being addressed to all people who will listen and respond to God: "Comfort . . . My people."

Those beginning verses look forward to a time when judgment will have ended, when Jerusalem will have paid enough for her iniquity. Young has pointed out that the three parts to the comfort of Jerusalem (v. 2) are developed in the three major sections in this part of the prophecy:

"Her warfare has ended" [40:1—48:22]
"Her iniquity has been removed" [49:1—57:21]
"She has received of the Lord's hand double for all her sin."
   [58:1—66:24][1]

1. Edward J. Young, *The Book of Isaiah* (NIC), 3:24.

To identify Jerusalem as the church, as Calvin and many other commentators do, is to depart from a literal hermeneutic. Jerusalem in its apostasy, degradation, and severe punishment is scarcely identified by anyone as the church. The prophet's message, as was seen at its beginning (1:1), was addressed primarily to the kingdom of Judah and specifically to the city of Jerusalem. Of course, that does not refer to the stone walls and buildings but to the people inhabiting the city. This is not the heavenly Jerusalem in which the church, along with other groups among God's people, has a part (Heb. 12:22-24), but the earthly city of Jerusalem. One certainly must recognize that the prophecy was not completely fulfilled by the return under Zerubbabel at the command of Cyrus. There is always in the picture the greater deliverance from sin and death through the greater "Anointed One."

The basis of the comfort is given in the next paragraph (vv. 3-5). The comfort is possible because of the Messiah, whose forerunner or herald is now introduced: "A voice is calling, 'Clear the way for the LORD in the wilderness; make smooth in the desert a highway for our God'" (v. 3).

The New Testament shows that this is a prophetic reference to John the Baptist (Baptizer), the forerunner of Christ (Matt. 3:3; Mark 1:3; Luke 3:4-6; John 1:23).

As always in the Old Testament prophetical books, the two comings of Christ are not distinguished but blended together. The prophecies of verses 4 and 5 were not completely fulfilled at His first advent. When He comes again there will be total fulfillment (cf. Rev. 1:7 with John 1:14; 2 Pet. 1:16-18; and 1 John 1:1-2).

The guarantee of the comfort that is promised is the Word of God in its everlastingness (vv. 6-8). Those words are alluded to in 1 Peter 1:24-25. The gospel shows up the frailty in man, but God's Word is sure and enduring.

The comfort is proclaimed in the announcement about the same One who earlier is called *Immanuel* ("God with us," Isa. 7:14; 8:8). Here the awe-inspiring statement is made: "Here is your God!" In verses 9-11 are seen both the strength and the tenderness of the Savior. His characterization as a shepherd is in harmony with the use of that as a title for God in a number of Old Testament passages (e.g., Pss. 23:1; 80:1; 95:7; 100:3) and foreshadows the application of that title by the Lord Jesus to Himself in John 10:11 (see also Heb. 13:20-21; 1 Pet. 2:25; 5:4).

THE CHARACTER AND OMNIPOTENCE OF GOD (40:12-31)

The chapter next contains a description of the character and omnipotence of God, abounding in rhetorical questions that awaken one to a sense of the Lord's almighty power (cf. Job 38). The questions, as in Job, are intended to put into the hearts of God's people an awareness of the infinite being and character of the Lord. Verse 12 emphasizes His omnipotence; that which no one else could do He can do. Verse 13 similarly stresses His omniscience. No one can inform God of anything, because He has always known everything.

Verse 15 goes back to a reminder of God's infinity. The nations, in contrast, are not only finite (even though made up of a multitude of individuals) but actually infinitesimal—"like a drop from a bucket" or "a speck of dust on the scales."

Passages such as this should give believers a solemn and joyous realization of God's majesty and glory. The tendency among many Christians today is to overstress the immanence of God with a practical neglect or even denial of the truth of His transcendence. Yes, God loves us and is our friend; but more than that He is our God, our sovereign Lord. We can love Him intimately but we must not consider ourselves on a level with Him, much less patronize Him as though we were giving Him the favor of our friendship. He is completely worthy of all our deepest adoration and worship.

"To whom then will you liken God?" (v. 18). How could He be compared with anyone, for He is the Creator and everyone and everything else is His created property? To compare God with anyone is to deny His infinite perfection. The question of verse 18 brings to light the absurdity of idolatry. For anyone to think he can make anything that would adequately represent God is utter folly, for God is the incomparable One. Verse 19 describes those who make metallic idols and verse 20 speaks of the procedure of one who is too poor to have an idol of gold or silver. The process of shaping a piece of wood into a "god" is described solemnly, but the satire is evident. The craftsman carefully carves and shapes the wood so that the "god" will have a firm base and will not be knocked over in the ordinary course of life.

The "vault" (NASB) or the "circle" (KJV) in verse 22 can refer either to the earth or to the heavens. At any rate, it emphasizes the immanence of God in His creation and refutes deism (the belief that God is the Creator but has no interest in or relationship to what He has made). Many writers have pointed out that this expression intimates, or at least does not rule out, the sphericity of the earth. The participial form is used, properly translated, "It is He who sits."

The question of verse 18 is repeated in the first person in verse 25 to emphasize again the impossibility of comparing God with anyone. The starry expanse is seen as evidence of His infinite power (v. 26). As we have built larger and greater telescopes, we have been able to see more of the immensity of the universe. Just to look at the stars with the unaided eye is awe-inspiring enough; one would think that the larger the vista the greater the awe, but unfortunately sin has blurred the effect. Instead of exclaiming at the almighty power of the Creator, people puff themselves up for being able to explore all those wonders. The fact remains that we cannot count the stars, but God knows all about each one. Verse 26 is like Psalm 19:1 and Romans 1:20 by asserting that the sight of our flaming universe ought to make people aware of the existence and power of God. Paul warns all that they are "without excuse" (Rom. 1:20).

The closing paragraph of the chapter (vv. 27-31) shows the strength of God by demonstrating that He is able to give strength to those who lack it. The titles used for God—"the Everlasting God, the Lord [Yahweh], the Creator of the ends of the earth"— make clear His omnipotence and omniscience and imply His omnipresence. What a comfort it is to the worn and fatigued believer to know that God never becomes weary or tired (v. 28). In human affairs, even those with the most strength sometimes find that strength depleted and reach out in their need to someone or something beyond themselves. Only God can help. Waiting for the Lord (v. 31) is literally "entwining oneself around the Lord." The word translated *gain* means literally to "change" or "exchange." The idea seems to be that such persons will exchange their worn-out, weakened condition for His strength. With Paul they can say, "I can do all things through Christ who strengthens me" (Phil. 4:13, NKJV*).

Mounting up "with wings like eagles" reminds one of those occasions of crisis or emergency when one needs exceptional power. Running also speaks of the spurts of energy needed for the exceptional exigencies. Walking describes the continuing, persis-

* *New King James Version.*

tent plodding that is necessary for consistent living for God. Perhaps men would have reversed that order, but the Holy Spirit is seemingly teaching that the persistent, consistent believer's living is the true climax requiring God's constant supply of strength. Another possibility is, as a number of commentators have suggested, that the sequence describes the various ages of a believer: the *soaring* representing the young in their strength; the *running*, those who are further along in life's path; and the *walking*, the steady pace of the older saint.

F. C. Jennings summarizes the passage in this way:

> Even the youths in the freshness of their morning powers succumb to weariness sooner or later, and eventually fall in utter weakness. But there are those who, while the strong are falling, still keep on their way without losing heart; or if at times their step, too, flags, lo, it is again renewed, and as though gifted with eagles' pinions, go on, their faith the wing that lifts them ever upward. Who are these thus blessed? They are those who wait on the Lord, owning their weakness, and drawing ever on the Lord Jesus, that limitless Source, for all that they lack, run without weariness, walk without fainting. May we each prove the truth of this in our journey through our one little life![2]

FURTHER PROOF OF THE LORD'S POWER AND DEITY (41:1-29)

In this section there is an emphasis on God's power as the guarantee of the deliverance of His people. Chapter 41 continues the thought of chapter 40 and gives further proof of the power of God as well as His deity—the fact that indeed He and He alone is God. In the *Ryrie Study Bible,* Charles Ryrie labels this whole section (chaps. 40-48) "The Greatness of God."[3]

In this chapter, God hurls a challenge at the idolatrous nations that are trusting in supposed "gods" to guide and deliver them. A contrast is drawn between the last verse of chapter 40 and the first verse of chapter 41. Those who wait on the Lord will renew *their* strength, but how are the idolaters to do so?

One should remember that the whole prophecy has to do primarily with the deliverance of Israel from Babylon. The human deliverer has not yet been named, but he now comes into view in 41:2—"one from the east." The *New American Standard Bible* is better here than the King James Version: "one from the east

---

2. F. C. Jennings, *Studies in Isaiah*, p. 476.
3. Charles C. Ryrie, *The Ryrie Study Bible* (NASB), p. 1069.

whom He calls in righteousness" rather than "the righteous man from the east." In spite of various attempts to make that refer to Abraham, Christ, Paul, and others, it seems most probable in this context that Cyrus is indicated, the Persian ruler who is specifically named in 44:28 and 45:1. God's hand is visibly manifest in history to those who are alive and alert enough to perceive it. The deliverer is seen as advancing into new territory, with God providentially delivering up nations before him. This is only one of many passages in the Old Testament that show the working of God in human history. In the light of the plain and extensive biblical teaching, the naturalistic historians are seen as having a woefully inadequate and unsatisfactory concept and philosophy of history. Who is it who performs and accomplishes these things? the Scripture repeats. Obviously, it is the sovereign God (v. 4).

The full meaning of the name (*Yahweh*, or traditionally, *Jehovah*) is unfolded here. Delitzsch comments:

> God is called Jehovah as the absolute I, the absolutely free Being, pervading all history, and yet above all history, as He who is Lord of His own absolute being, in revealing which He is purely self-determined; in a word, as the unconditionally free and unchangeably eternal personality.[4]

The idolatrous nations are pictured as bolstering up their "gods" (idols) to try to withstand the invasion (vv. 5-7). There is sarcasm in this description of the plight of the idolaters. They encourage one another to work faster and faster, turning out more gods to "help" them.

The attention now shifts from the idolatrous nations to the nation of Israel, which God addresses directly in verse 8 and calls His "servant." This is the first mention of the servant in Isaiah, a theme that recurs several times. In passages such as this one the term is applied to the whole nation of Israel; in others it refers to the nucleus of the nation, the godly remnant; and in still others, to an individual—the Messiah. Many students of the Old Testament, especially those among the Jewish people, have failed to recognize those differences. As Delitzsch and others point out, this passage is filled with deep affection: "Israel, My servant, Jacob whom I have chosen, descendant of Abraham My friend" (v. 8).

4. Franz Delitzsch, *Biblical Commentary on the Prophecies of Isaiah*, 2:160.

God's sovereign election of Israel, mentioned in other places in the Scriptures, is prominent here (cf. Deut. 14:2). Because the people were chosen in Abraham, the geographic references here must be to Ur and Mesopotamia.

God's choice is stated first affirmatively, then negatively: "I have chosen you and not rejected you" (v. 9). No matter how much Gentile rulers and others may rail against that doctrine and deny it, God does have a chosen nation, as both the Old Testament and the New Testament frequently and emphatically affirm. In fact, a person's theology can often be distinguished by his answer to the simple but crucial question: Does Israel as a nation have a future? Those who spiritualize the Old Testament promises and give them all to the church must answer no to be consistent.

One must make a distinction, however, between interpretation and application. The promise of verse 10 in its context refers to Israel, but the analogy of faith or the wider context of Scripture as a whole informs us that such a promise can be appropriated by any believing child of God in any age or dispensation (see Eph. 1:3). Discernment is essential.

In contrast, God has never promised Gentiles one square foot of the land of Canaan, Palestine, or Israel to have for their possession, but He did promise the whole land to Abraham, Isaac, Jacob, and their descendants. Nevertheless, a Christian under grace can appropriate the spiritual promises of the Old Testament (Eph. 1:3).

The verbs in verse 10 show what God habitually does for His people. He acts in righteousness in upholding them. The word order here "heaps one synonym upon another, expressive of the divine love . . . Language is too contracted to hold all [its] fulness."[5]

Verses 11 and 12 show the two parts of the picture. God's help to Israel spells the doom and punishment of Israel's enemies. This picture with its two sides is seen throughout the prophetic Word. Some nations are going to be brought to nothingness, to complete desolation. Verse 13 gives the reason for the overcoming of the enemies.

Jacob (not the individual but the nation descended from him) is addressed in verse 14 as a "worm," not to indicate worthlessness in God's sight but weakness and helplessness in the eyes of the

5. Ibid., 2:164.

nations. That is how Israel would really be apart from God's electing love, but He promises to make the nation "a new, sharp threshing sledge with double edges" (v. 15). Restored Israel will become an instrument of judgment to the nations of the world, which in turn will be scattered (v. 16).

Water (as in v. 17) is so often used in Scripture as a symbol of blessing because it satisfies the burning thirst acquired in a sunny, hot area. The promise of verse 18 is reminiscent of chapter 35 (cf. Jer. 12:12). Seven trees are enumerated as the result of that divine irrigation (v. 19), probably indicating the perfection of that undertaking by God. The synonyms for perception (v. 20) show the great force of the impression that will be made. Those who have true knowledge will know and acknowledge that God is responsible. The last verb in the sentence—"has created"—is stronger than the previous synonym. God not only will have done that, but in doing it will have produced a new result.

In the latter part of the chapter (beginning with v. 21) the challenge implied at the beginning is brought out in detail. It is a call to the idols to prophesy. One of the great motifs of Isaiah is that only the Lord (Yahweh) can foretell the future, and His doing so proves that He *is* God. Prediction of the future is the prerogative of God alone because He and He only is the all-knowing One. That fact is asserted often in Isaiah. Prophecy is the seal of authentication that God has placed on His Word to show its genuineness.

"Present your case" (v. 21) is a technical phrase introducing a lawsuit. The One who calls for the suit is the "King of Jacob." The false gods and their followers (v. 22) are challenged to compete with the Lord in history and prophecy. God has placed Himself in contrast to the pagans and their deities. To prove their deity the idols would have to speak, but not only do they not speak; they *cannot speak*. The contemptuous conclusion is voiced in verse 24: "Behold, you are of no account, and your work amounts to nothing; He who chooses you is an abomination."

In verse 25, after that awesome confrontation, the prophet goes back to the thought of verse 2, again mentioning the coming deliverer from the Babylonian captivity. He was said to be from the east, and here the sun rising is mentioned. Why is he identified as from the north? Only those familiar with the geography of the region—including what the historian Breasted named the "Fertile Crescent"—can see that there is no contradiction. The realm of the Medes and the Persians was indeed to the east of the land of Israel, but because of the desert any invaders from the east would have to enter Israel from the north, taking a route that would first proceed northwest and then southward.

None of the individual idols or all of them together can prevent God's fulfillment of that tremendous prophecy, for they are nonentities. The conclusion of the section comes in verses 28 and 29. God's challenge has gone by default, so to speak, for no one has answered Him. Both the idols and their worshipers stand condemned. "Their works" (v. 29) refer to the idols themselves (cf. Ps. 115:4-8).

THE LORD'S SERVANT WHO WILL BRING JUDGMENT (42:1-9)

Chapter 42 is clearly a messianic passage. Much of the same thought is developed later in chapters 49 and 53 concerning the Servant. In the first nine verses of this chapter the Lord Jesus Christ is seen in His relationship to the Gentiles.

The "behold" of 41:29 and the "behold" of 42:1 are in sharp contrast. God is saying, "Look at My Servant, the antithesis of the false gods." The characterization of Christ as the Servant of Yahweh, first brought out in Isaiah, is expanded in the gospels, especially in Mark, which shows a close connection with Isaiah, and is also recognized by the church in the book of Acts (3:13; 4:27, 30).

One should remember that previously (41:8) the nation is called the Lord's servant. But 42:1 is obviously different. The passage is clearly referring to an individual, and the New Testament use of it is conclusive in referring it to the Lord Jesus Christ. Delitzsch says:

> The Servant of Jehovah who is presented to us here is distinct from Israel, and has so strong an individuality and such marked personal features that the expression cannot possibly be merely a personified collective. Nor can the prophet himself be intended; for what is here affirmed of the servant of Jehovah goes infinitely beyond anything to which a prophet was ever called, or of which a man was ever capable. It must therefore be the future Christ; and this is the view taken in the Targum.[6]

Isaiah 42:1-4 is quoted in Matthew 12:17-21 where the ministry of the Lord Jesus Christ is said to be the fulfillment of the

6. Ibid., 2:174.

prophecy. It should be noted again, however, that the two advents of Christ are as usual mingled together. There is the ministry of Christ in weakness and the ministry of Christ in power; the despised and rejected Christ and the conquering and judging Christ.

Verse 2 expresses the mild demeanor of the Lord Jesus (cf. Matt. 11:28-30). He is unostentatious, not sensational. The passage looks forward to the complete accomplishment of His purposes. Yahweh's announcement to His Servant is echoed in other passages, particularly in chapter 61, as will be seen.

The reference to "those who dwell in darkness" and the "prison" (v. 7) alludes to spiritual evil. That figure is often employed in Scripture, and the gospels so interpret it. The import of verse 8 is that God is pledging His own name; that is, His honor, that the work mentioned here will be accomplished by His Servant. The sacred name—Yahweh—is used with emphasis here. No other "god" is ever given that name in Scripture. It is the distinctive personal name for the one true, living God. Because God is who He is and what He is, His absolute holiness demands that He not be deprived of the honor that is rightfully His due. He not only will not, but cannot, surrender His glory to any other being.

In verse 9 the Lord appeals on the ground of fulfilled prophecy to His people's faith to be reposed in prophecies that are yet unfulfilled.

In contrast to the destructive, critical view that sees the ancient Israelites as entirely selfish in their concept of God, the reality is shown here: a recognition that the salvation brought by the Messiah will extend to the Gentiles (note particularly v. 6). This is not the first time that truth has been enunciated in Isaiah (cf. chap. 9), nor is it by any means the last.

The challenge to the idols that has been seen in the previous chapter is carried on throughout this section. Babylon, the center and hotbed of idolatry, is to be destroyed. God is going to see to it that idols do not get the glory that rightfully belongs to Him.

THE POWER OF GOD MANIFEST THROUGH HIS SERVANT (42:10-25)

With the call to sing a new song (v. 10) comes a declaration of the power of God, which is manifested through His Servant the Messiah. The song is comparable to the exquisite song of salvation in chapter 12.

The chapter closes with a rebuke of Israel for unfaithfulness. The true explanation for the Babylonian captivity is seen in passages such as this one. God in righteousness must visit judgment on His people for their sins. Babylon, although exceedingly powerful as compared to the relatively tiny kingdom of Judah, could not have inflicted what it did on Judah apart from the permissive will of God. The theme of God's punishment of His wicked people by means of an even more wicked people is found in a number of the prophets, notably in Habakkuk (see Hab. 1:5-11).

ISRAEL'S PRIVILEGE AND RESPONSIBILITY AS GOD'S SERVANT
(43:1-28)

In this chapter (a part of the section on the deliverance from Babylon) we see Israel's privilege and responsibility as God's servant. Addressing the people of Israel, God reminds them that He has chosen them. A number of times He uses the name *Jacob* as well as the new name *Israel* as a designation for the nation, which must leave its Jacob-characteristics and become truly Israel. God's calling Israel by name (v. 1) shows the special relationship He established with the people of that nation by covenant. Israel belongs to Him in a special sense. Consequently, He will accomplish her ultimate good. That is a constantly reiterated marvel of God's grace found in Scripture. God bears a special relationship to Israel, not only as Creator, but also as Savior and Redeemer. The title the "Holy One of Israel," used in both major parts of Isaiah, shows that special relationship.

The experiences described in verse 2 have no doubt been encountered in numerous ways by the people of God in various generations. There was a literal fulfillment of the last part of verse 2 in the experience of Daniel's three friends—Hananiah, Mishael, and Azariah—in the fiery furnace in Babylon (Dan. 3:1-30).

The language of verse 5 and following seems to contain that familiar combination of the near view and the far view observed in various parts of Isaiah. There undoubtedly is allusion to the return (or strictly speaking, *the returns*) from Babylonian captivity (Ezra 2:1-70; 7:1-10; Neh. 2:1-10), but there is also the recognition of a later return from all parts of the earth ("from afar" and "from the ends of the earth") in verse 6.

The servant character of the nation of Israel is emphasized in verse 10. The Old Testament views Israel as a channel of God's blessing to the whole world. Israel in itself was largely a failure, but it is yet to be such a channel. Paul emphasizes that in Romans 11, showing how Israel's failure was overruled by God to bring blessings to the Gentiles in the church, but that even greater blessing will come to the nations of the world when Israel is restored in God's good time.

In verses 11-17 God reminds His people of His past intervention for them. Just as He delivered them at the Red Sea in the time of Moses (v. 16), so He will deliver them now. In fact, the new deliverance by God will so overshadow the old that the "former things" will not be remembered (vv. 18-20).

"Yet," in spite of all God has done and all that He is capable of doing, "you have not called on Me," God says (v. 22). The grace of God stands out in all its brilliance when compared with the ingratitude of Israel. God formed Israel for Himself (v. 21) and longed for fellowship, but Israel did not call on Him. Instead, Israel wearied God with her iniquities (v. 24). Judgment must come because of the nation's sins; nevertheless God is the One who forgives sin (v. 25).

THE POWERFUL GOD AND THE POWERLESS IDOLS (44:1-28)

In chapter 44, at the heart of the nine-chapter section (40-48) on the deliverance of Israel, God's promises to Israel are seen again. He can fulfill those promises because He is the all-powerful God as contrasted with the powerless idols. The promises are not based on what Israel has done or will do, but on what God *has* done by His own love and grace. Twice He speaks of Israel as His "chosen." On the second occasion He used the symbolic name *Jeshurun* ("Upright," v. 2), which He had used in Deuteronomy 32:15 and 33:5, 26. That is the genius of the Word of God—one part alludes to other parts so that the person who is making a continual study of Scripture is always being amazed and delighted at the new connections, the new parallels, the new glimpses of truth placed there by the infinitely wise Author.

"I will pour out water on the thirsty land" (v. 3). That often-repeated figure is used here to portray the Holy Spirit's blessing on what would otherwise be barren ground. As noted previously, water is particularly appropriate as a symbol of God's spiritual blessings.

Again God mentions His omniscience as the proof that He can fulfill His promises (vv. 6-8). It is perhaps hard for today's reader to see the point of some of these allusions. One needs to realize that the people of Israel lived in an almost completely idolatrous environment and that Israel was a little island of monotheism in a great sea of polytheism. Worse than that, Israel was not even what God wanted her to be, for a great many of the people of Israel in Isaiah's day were idolaters. Even Hezekiah's reforms did not permanently affect the mass of the kingdom of Judah. Consequently, most of the people knew from first-hand experience what an idol was. The tragedy was that many, who by position ought to have been examples for the people of God, were making and falling down before idols.

That explains the relevancy of the magnificent satire (vv. 9-20). It is always a source of astonishment that men would attribute supernatural powers to something they had fashioned with their own hands. Isaiah paints a picture of a man who uses part of a log to warm himself and to cook his food, and then makes another part of the same piece of wood into a "god" (vv. 15-17). Of course, practically all idolaters, ancient and modern, have maintained that they do not worship the image but only what is represented by the image. In reality most of them, whether they acknowledge it or not, are worshiping the image; and even if they are not, they are not worshiping the one true and living God, who is Spirit (John 4:24) and cannot be represented by any image or likeness of anything.

Yet again, beginning with verse 21, is heard the glorious strain of a song of redemption for Israel. It is a song unconfined, a song of heaven and earth. God says to Jerusalem, which certainly was inhabited in Isaiah's time but which was to become uninhabited and desolate in the Babylonian captivity, "She shall be inhabited!" (v. 26).

Finally, God mentions the man who is to be His instrument of deliverance from the Babylonian exile: "It is I who says of Cyrus, 'He is My shepherd! And he will perform all My desire.' And he declares of Jerusalem, 'She will be built,' And of the temple, 'Your foundation will be laid'" (v. 28).

That is actually the crux of the critics' problem about the book of Isaiah. Here Isaiah in the eighth century B.C. announces Cyrus, who lived in the sixth century B.C., as the restorer of the people to Jerusalem. This is not the only place, however, where God has named a man long before his birth. For example, there was a similar prophecy about Josiah almost three centuries before his time (1 Kings 13:2).

The whole thrust of the passage is that God, who is omniscient, is the One who is announcing events beforehand. That is proof of His deity. Destructive critics who say this passage must have been written in the sixth century by some otherwise unknown prophet in Babylon ("Deutero-Isaiah") are making the same mistake that the idolaters in Isaiah's day were making. They are also like the Sadducees of another time, to whom the Lord Jesus Christ said, "You are mistaken, not understanding the Scriptures, or the power of God" (Matt. 22:29).

The historical fulfillment of this prophecy is told in 2 Chronicles 36:22-23 and Ezra 1:1-11. Cyrus gave the decree for the rebuilding of the Temple in Jerusalem in 538 B.C., almost two hundred years after this prophecy.

GOD'S PURPOSES THROUGH CYRUS, HIS ANOINTED (45:1-25)

In chapter 45 God reveals His purposes through Cyrus, whom He calls His "anointed." This chapter, of course, is very closely related to the preceding one. In 44:28 Cyrus is introduced and described in the third person. In 45:1 and the following verses he is addressed directly in the second person. There is in these opening verses a prophetic statement of Cyrus's victories (vv. 1-8).

Cyrus is the only Gentile king who is called in Scripture God's "anointed." This is the translation of the Hebrew word normally rendered in English as *messiah*. Thus, Cyrus becomes in a sense a type of *the Messiah,* the Anointed One, the Lord Jesus Christ Himself.

Typology is often misunderstood and abused. Some people deny the existence of types altogether and some go to the other extreme, as was said of some of the early church writers, that they made every stick of wood in the Old Testament a type of the cross!

A type is a divinely appointed prophetic symbol, usually a symbol of Christ. When a person or a thing is called a type, that does not alter its literal meaning or deny its historical reality. Cyrus was a Persian king, not an Israelite, and there is no evidence that he ever really knew the true God. In fact, God says, "You have not known Me" (45:4). Consequently, if one calls Cyrus a type of the Lord Jesus Christ, one is not saying he is like the Lord Jesus Christ in every respect (that would be blasphemy). The type is strictly limited. The only intended resemblance is in the fact that Cyrus was anointed by God to deliver the people of Israel from the Babylonian captivity. As such he points, without any intention on his part, to the greater Anointed One who is the Deliverer from a far worse captivity—the captivity of sin and Satan.

Although Cyrus did not know God (v. 4), God used him to work out His purposes for His people Israel. It will come undoubtedly as a shock to many people to discover that God in His sovereign providence regulates the affairs of mighty nations, such as Babylon and the Medo-Persian Empire, for the welfare of the widely despised and ridiculed people of Israel. Although Cyrus did not know it, it was God who enabled him to destroy the power of the Babylonian Empire. The transition of power from Babylon to the Medes and the Persians is seen in the book of Daniel, written by Daniel who lived at that time.

After the recital of the victories of Cyrus, God again reverts to the theme of His salvation of Israel (vv. 9-17). He speaks of an "everlasting salvation" (v. 17), and the word *everlasting* is a cue to the fact that He has more in store for His people than deliverance from Babylon, wonderful as that will be. Cyrus the "messiah" is only a temporary shadow; Jesus Christ, *the Messiah*, is the eternal reality.

Here again, however, the message is clearly expounded that salvation through the Messiah is not to be restricted to the nation of Israel. Isaiah uses the expression that some may sometimes use without awareness of its origin: "The ends of the earth" (v. 22). The poor deluded idolaters of the Gentiles will yet be visited with the salvation of the Lord (Yahweh). Messiah will yet reign in universal righteousness and peace. God's oath that all will someday be in subjection to Him will be fulfilled: "That to Me every knee will bow, every tongue will swear allegiance" (v. 23).

The New Testament echoes of that statement are not hard to find. The verse is directly quoted in Romans 14:11 and is most certainly alluded to in the great passage on the person of Christ in Philippians 2:10-11:

> That at the name of Jesus every knee should bow, of things in heaven, and things in earth, and things under the earth; and that every tongue should confess that Jesus Christ is Lord, to the glory of God the Father. [KJV]

JUDGMENT ON BABYLON'S IDOLS (46:1-13)

The judgment that God was to bring on the Babylonian Empire was described in the first part of Isaiah as the first of the oracles or burdens of the Gentile nations (Isa. 13). In that passage Babylon was seen with other nations in a general view of Gentile judgment. At this point the prophecy gives more particulars about the judgment on Babylon, the great oppressor of the people of Judah. The judgment is viewed not only as something coming on Babylon itself, but also as an object lesson for Israel. It is only fitting that Babylon's downfall should be seen in connection with the deliverance of Israel, which is the general theme of this section (chaps. 40-48) and inevitably had to include Babylon's defeat and destruction.

Judgment on Babylon also means judgment on Babylon's gods (vv. 1-2). Bel and Nebo were two of the leading gods of Babylon. This is indeed a graphic scene, depicting the confusion and rout brought about by the Medo-Persian conquest. Babylon's idols, unable to protect and defend her, are themselves being carried into captivity. The scene is laughable for anyone who has a sense of humor. These are *gods* bouncing and jolting along on the beasts of burden?

A decided contrast comes at the beginning of verse 3. God says in effect to Israel, "These gods of Babylon have to be carried if they are going anywhere, but *I* am the One who has carried *you*." God's providential care of His own extends from birth until death; He and His blessings are unchanging and continuous.

The theme of comparison—or rather, the impossibility of comparison—recurs in verses 5-7. One may wonder why God keeps bringing up that subject. No doubt it is because His people are so slow to learn. The psalmist rehearses the taunts of the pagan neighbors of Israel as they exclaim in effect, "We can see *our* gods; here they are; but you have a God you cannot see. Where is He?" The answer of the true believer is steadfast: "But our God is in the heavens; He does whatever He pleases (Ps. 115:3).

Isaiah's conclusion is the same as that of the psalmist; "Though one may cry to it, it cannot answer; it cannot deliver him from his distress (v. 7).

Babylon's multitudinous pantheon cannot ward off the Persian power because the gods are nonentities. Consequently, the Lord's purpose will be fulfilled. Part of the good pleasure of God (vv. 10-11) is to call Cyrus and enable him to accomplish the destruction of the Babylonian Empire. Here he is called a "bird of prey from the east," but he is also called, "the man of My purpose from a far country" (v. 11). The fact that the Lord not only knew all about that but also announced it ahead of time exhibits for all to see His existence and deity. God is the only One who can declare the end from the beginning, and His declaring of that is, as Isaiah had previously stated, the proof of who and what He is. When the events come to pass, then men can learn of the Lord's omniscience and omnipotence.

All of this constitutes a warning to transgressors as God severely admonishes them to listen to Him (vv. 12-13). His salvation "will not delay." God's timetable of events is sure. Peter reminds us that God "is not slow about His promise" (2 Pet. 3:9).

JUDGMENT ON THE BABYLONIAN EMPIRE (47:1-15)

At the beginning of chapter 47 Babylon is pictured as a young woman who is being put in a position of disgrace and shame: "Sit on the ground without a throne" (v. 1).

This chapter should be compared with what has already been said in chapters 13 and 14. This Babylonian Empire, sometimes called in history the Neo-Babylonian or Chaldean Empire, reached its height under Nebuchadnezzar, who captured and destroyed the city of Jerusalem in 586 B.C. At the time Isaiah prophesied, that was naturally in the future.

The book of Daniel describes conditions during the time of Nebuchadnezzar and afterward. Chapter 5 of Daniel records the fulfillment of the prophecy given in Isaiah 47, when the city of Babylon was captured by the army of the Medes and Persians.

Claiming to be the "queen of kingdoms" (v. 5), Babylon was used by God as an instrument of judgment on His own people Israel. Now Babylon is to be judged, not because of some arbitrary notion on God's part, but because Babylon is sinful and richly deserves the judgment. Although this is a judgment on historical Babylon, one may also note (as many have pointed out) that Babylon in Scripture is sometimes symbolic of mankind in organized rebellion against God. That is certainly the force of the term in the book of Revelation. From Genesis 11 on, Babylon (Babel) has manifested this character.

Babylon "felt secure in . . . wickedness and said, 'No one sees me'" (v. 10). God has abundant reason for judgment. The principle of God's using a sinful nation to punish another sinful nation is observed in other prophetical books besides Isaiah. Jeremiah and Habakkuk particularly speak of it (e.g., Jer. 25:1-11; Hab. 1:12—2:1).

Babylon was teeming with all kinds of idols, pagan priests, astrologers, soothsayers, charlatans, and demon-inspired religionists. But not one of them was able to help. They too were to be destroyed. No doubt from a human point of view there was much that was admirable in the achievements of the Babylonians. They had a relatively high state of civilization, grand buildings, and a seemingly impregnable city. They were advanced in mathematics, astronomy, and literature. But the moral character of the empire was such that the people of God need not shed a tear over its downfall. In the book of Revelation, God calls on His people to rejoice, not to mourn as He announces the complete destruction of the world-system, symbolically called Babylon.

EXHORTATIONS TO THE IMPENITENT AND UNBELIEVING (48:1-22)

Instead of being concerned about the downfall of Babylon, Israel should have been concerned about its own relationship to God. Chapter 48 contains exhortations to the impenitent and unbelieving. God has made known the things that were to come. Had His people profited from that revelation?

The people, as has been seen from the beginning of Isaiah, have given lip service to the Lord while continuing to practice idolatry. The picture that God paints of Israel in these verses is far from a flattering one: "not in truth nor in righteousness" (v. 1); "obstinate" (v. 4); dealing "very treacherously" (v. 8). God addresses the nation as Jacob because that side of their ancestor's character was more prominent than the "Israel" side. God continues His gracious appeal that His people listen to Him (v. 12). This is one of the great passages in the Scripture that show the practical purpose and effect of prophecy. It is something that many of God's people today do not yet understand—the practical nature of prophecy. There are some who study the details of prophecy simply because they find a fascination in the subject. They are intrigued by it as if it were a cleverly constructed puzzle to be solved. They have missed the point. Prophecy ought to have some effect on a Christian's daily walk.

"If only you had paid attention to My commandments!" The Lord exclaims. "Then your well-being would have been like a river" (v. 18).

Seeing God's sovereign control of history ought to solemnize any individual, so that one would give one's life to Him; so that one should recognize God's complete right to everyone.

This section emphasizes the almighty power of God in contrast to the idols. It closes with the admonition to God's people to disassociate themselves from the evil Babylon (v. 20) and to accept the salvation or deliverance of God. Finally, there is the solemn warning: "No peace . . . for the wicked" (v. 22), a refrain that marks off the sections and is encountered again at the end of chapter 57.

9

The Suffering Servant as the Redeemer

$(49:1 — 57:21)$

The middle section of the three that make up the second part of Isaiah centers on the Messiah as the suffering Servant of the Lord. This is Christ the Redeemer. The section may be outlined as follows:

II. The Suffering Servant as the Redeemer (49:1—57:21)
   A. God's Salvation Through the Servant (49:1-26)
   B. Exhortations to the Unbelieving (50:1-11)
   C. Exhortations to the Righteous (51:1-23)
   D. Zion's Joy in the Lord's Deliverance (52:1-12)
   E. The Suffering Servant of the Lord (52:13—53:12)
   F. Restoration of Israel to the Place of Blessing (54:1-17)
   G. Appeal to Come to God for Salvation (55:1-13)
   H. Moral Exhortations in View of God's Salvation (56:1-12)
   I. Contrast of the Contrite and the Wicked (57:1-21)

While the idea of the servant is constantly changing, sometimes referring to Israel and sometimes to the Messiah, this section emphasizes the messianic aspect. Messiah was introduced as the Servant in the previous section (Isa. 42), but here His person and work are more clearly set forth.

GOD'S SALVATION THROUGH THE SERVANT (49:1-26)

As chapter 49 opens, the Messiah is speaking. The first half of the chapter tells of the exaltation of Messiah (vv. 1-13); the second half, of the glory that is to come to Zion (vv. 14-26). Even though the speaker is called "Israel" in verse 4, the context shows it is obviously not the nation that is speaking. The description is individualistic. As many commentators have asserted, the Servant of this passage is the Immanuel of 7:14. Charles Ryrie says:

> Here the Messiah (cf. 41:8; 42:1), called *Israel* because in Him alone all of God's expectations were realized (49:3). His mission is to restore Israel to God and to bring *light* to the Gentiles (v. 6). Though *despised* at His first coming, He will be worshiped at His second coming (v. 7).[1]

Taking up an idea that has been given before (45:22), God says to the Servant: "I will also make You a light of the nations so that My salvation may reach to the end of the earth" (v. 6).

Through that marvelous salvation Zion is to be comforted. Zion is a title used often in Scripture for the city of Jerusalem and was originally the hill on which the ancient citadel was erected. In her captivity and judgment Zion is tempted to think that God has forgotten and forsaken her (v. 14), but He assures her that that cannot be (vv. 15-16). In glorifying Israel God will make use of Gentiles and will hold to a strict accounting all those who have oppressed His people (v. 26).

EXHORTATIONS TO THE UNBELIEVING (50:1-11)

In chapter 50, which contains exhortations to the unbelieving, God draws a contrast between the submissive Servant and disobedient Israel. In the opening paragraph He shows His people that He has not rejected them, but that their sufferings arise from their own sins (vv. 1-3). God asks, "Why was there no man when I came?" (v. 2). He "came" by His servants the prophets (cf. Heb. 1:1) and later by the Servant Himself, His beloved Son (cf. Heb. 1:2; John 1:10-11), but Israel did not give the proper response. Even when Christ came, He was rejected.

The next paragraph (vv. 4-9) amplifies the thought of the opposition to the Lord's Servant (cf. Heb. 12:4). In verse 4, the King James Version is better than the *New American Standard Bible*—"the tongue of the learned."

It is not Isaiah who is speaking in this passage, nor is it an idealized portrait of the nation of Israel. It is an individual, not a

---

1. Charles C. Ryrie, *The Ryrie Study Bible* (NASB), p. 1086.

group; it is *the Servant*, the Lord Jesus Christ. He says: "I gave My back to those who strike Me, and My cheeks to those who pluck out the beard; I did not cover My face from humiliation and spitting" (v. 6). That verse finds its historical fulfillment in the accounts in the gospels of the sufferings of Christ (see Matt. 26:67; 27:30). The Servant allowed Himself to be made subject to the worst indignities. He did not hide His face in confusion (contrast Jer. 51:51). Comparison of those with other passages shows the applicability of Isaiah's prophecy to the Lord Jesus Christ exclusively.

In verse 7 the Servant rests His case with God and goes forward with unflinching determination—what Stier called the "holy hardness of endurance." That same expression is found in the Greek text of Luke 9:51 (cf. Ezek. 3:8-9). "I know that I shall not be ashamed," He says, because He is free from real dishonor; everything that He endures is vicarious. How wonderful that He was willing to undergo all that for our salvation!

The Servant proceeds to show that He is not discouraged, because His justifier is near. The word translated "He who vindicates Me" is a legal term (cf. Deut. 25:1). God will declare Him just, free from all the accusations of His enemies. Who is able to enter into a legal controversy with the Servant when God Himself is the Judge? (Cf. 41:1, 21; 43:9, 26; 45:20; 48:14, 16).

The chapter closes with the mention of two ways: the way of trust (v. 10) and the way of sorrow (v. 11); that is, dependence on God or dependence on self. The first way leads to peace and salvation, the other to destruction. Those are in essence the same two ways presented in Psalm 1 and in the words of the Lord Jesus Christ in His Sermon on the Mount (Matt. 7:13-14).

In the closing verse the Lord is speaking to the nation and telling them that what they have prepared for the Servant will be the means of their own punishment. "The fire of wrath becomes the fire of divine judgment, and this fire becomes their bed of torment"[2]

EXHORTATIONS TO THE RIGHTEOUS (51:1-23)

It might be said that the previous exhortations were addressed to the nation as a whole, whereas these in chapter 51 are addressed

2. Franz Delitzsch, *Biblical Commentary on the Prophecies of Isaiah*, 2:281.

to the godly remnant, those "who pursue righteousness" (v. 1). The first part of the chapter gives comforting assurances to those who seek the Lord (vv. 1-16); the remainder again speaks of the triumph of Jerusalem and the destruction of her enemies (vv. 17-23).

The exhortation of verse 1 is for those who sustain the proper relationship to God, in contrast to the wicked of 46:12 and chapters 48 and 50. The "rock" and the "quarry" are figurative expressions for their extraction or descent. The righteous are exhorted to look to those who have gone before, their ancestors or progenitors.

In verse 2 the figure of the preceding verse is stated literally with the mention of Abraham and Sarah. Abraham, as the ancestor of the nation of Israel, is mentioned one hundred fifteen times in the Bible in addition to the numerous times he is named in Genesis, but Sarah is referred to only a few times. Emphasis is placed here on the fact that Abraham was only one when God called him. The contrast is between the *one* and the word *multiplied* (cf. Gen. 15:5 and Ezek. 33:24). The increase given by God as described in verse 2 looks forward to what is said in the next verse about the fulfillment of God's promises. The promise-keeping God will fulfill His word even more abundantly in the future.

The statement at the beginning of verse 3 looks back to the opening note of this part of Isaiah (40:1). The change that is to come on the land is set forth in very strong language (cf. Ezek. 31:9). "As Sarah gave birth to Isaac after a long period of barrenness, so Zion, a second Sarah, will be surrounded by a joyous multitude of children after a long period of desolation."[3]

The words *righteousness* and *salvation* in verse 5 are used synonymously (cf. 46:13). There is salvation for God's people at the same time as there is judgment on His enemies. "My arms" is an allusion to God's power, as in verse 9 and in 53:1.

In verse 9 an appeal is made that Yahweh's power may be exerted on Israel's behalf. There is reference to the manifested power of God in the deliverance from Egypt (represented here by the term *rahab*) and in the further deliverance at the Red Sea (v. 10). It is followed by the same joyous refrain found previously in 35:10. Characteristic repetitions in Isaiah, such as the inter-

3. Ibid., 2:283.

weaving of themes and refrains and reappearances of leading ideas, help to show the perfect unity of the book.

The same God who created the heavens and divided the sea for Israel in her earlier history will bring about this glorious deliverance. Jerusalem, who has drunk the cup of God's fury to the dregs, has the promise that she will never drink of it again (v. 22). Instead, the oppressors of Israel shall drink of it (v. 23).

ZION'S JOY IN THE LORD'S DELIVERANCE (52:1-12)

This chapter portrays Zion's joy in the Lord's deliverance. Again (as in 51:17) Jerusalem is called on to awaken (v. 1). The city is pictured as a beautiful woman who has been prostrate in the dust, but who is now to get up and sit on the throne that God has prepared for her (v. 2). Sitting or lying in the dust indicates her mourning and the fact that she had been a prisoner.

God is the One who delivers. "Since God had received no price for them, He was under no obligation to release them."[4] God is pictured here as absolute. He is sovereign and in need of nothing, but able to give all things on behalf of His people. Verse 4 lists the oppressions of Israel by Egypt, Assyria, and Babylon. The rulers mentioned in verse 5 are the pagan oppressors who exult cruelly over the plight of Israel and blaspheme the name of God, which is deserving of the highest honor. God presents Himself as the One who is true and omnipotent in fulfilling His promise of redemption (v. 6).

The herald is next pictured as coming on the mountains around Jerusalem to proclaim God's salvation and reign (v. 7). Paul makes an application of this in reference to the gospel in Romans 10:15. The "watchmen" (v. 8) are the prophets, as in other passages (cf. 56:10; Jer. 6:17; Ezek. 3:17; 33:2, 7).

The baring of God's holy arm (v. 10) is a reference to the practice in ancient warfare of going into battle with the right arm unencumbered. The result of the display of God's power will be to convince the nations so that "all the ends of the earth may see the salvation of our God" (v. 10).

Verses 11 and 12 describe the going out from Babylon. There is a parallel in the mystical Babylon of the end time, as God's people

---

4. Joseph Addison Alexander, *Commentary on the Prophecies of Isaiah*, 2:274.

are commanded to come out of the evil world-system (Rev. 18:4-5). This going out is in contrast to the Exodus from Egypt, on which occasion the Israelites were told to ask for possessions from the Egyptians to recompense them for the many years of slavery they had endured (see Ex. 12:36). The mention of the vessels of the Lord (v. 11) "is an indirect prophecy, and was fulfilled in the fact that Cyrus directed the gold and silver vessels," which Nebuchadnezzar had stolen from the Temple and taken to Babylon, "to be restored to the returning exiles as their rightful property (Ezra 1:7-11)."[5]

The fact that they were not to go out in haste is also in contrast to the departure from Egypt (Ex. 12:11). In the last sentence of Isaiah 52:12 is evidently an allusion to the pillar of cloud (cf. Ex. 14:19-20).

It is as though a complete cycle has been made from chapter 40, for the message again is related that "the LORD has comforted His people" (v. 9). With the Lord both before and behind them, Israel is safe (v. 12).

Needless to say, commentators who are amillennial in their eschatology and those who do not have a dispensational viewpoint regard Jerusalem or Zion as the church and find a "spiritual" meaning as the only valid extension of the prophecy. Some, of course, take the position that the return from Babylon in Cyrus's day or a later period exhausts the prophecies. They will not, or cannot, see national Israel as having any part in the future. The return from Babylon was a fulfillment of prophecy both in Isaiah and in other books; there is no doubt about that. But Scripture also abounds in predictions concerning the worldwide restoration of the people of Israel to their own land in the end time.

This commentary has said repeatedly that the deliverance through Cyrus is a foreshadowing of a greater deliverance through the Messiah. That does not rule out *application* of those great spiritual truths to all believers of every age or dispensation. How thankful New Testament saints can and should be to God for including them in so many of His great promises! *Principles* that apply to Israel in the Old Testament can be seen as applying to the church in the New Testament. But Israel is Israel, Jerusalem is Jerusalem, Zion is Zion, and to call any of those entities the

5. Delitzsch, 2:301.

church, as the Reformers (great men and Bible scholars though they were) did and as so many of their followers do, is to introduce hopeless confusion to the interpretation of Scripture. Some segments of the church that are ready to claim *all* of Israel's physical and material blessings as well as the spiritual ones are not so ready to accept God's judgments and curses on Israel. The church is never called Israel in the New Testament. Paul's reference to "the Israel of God" in Galatians 6:16 is evidently to the true Israel, the godly remnant, who during this present church age are a part of the church, as Paul himself was (Rom. 11:1-6). The New Testament recognizes three ethnic divisions of mankind: "Jews," "Greeks" [that is, Gentiles], and "the church of God" (1 Cor. 10:32). That last group contains those believers in Christ from both Jewish and Gentile backgrounds.

We may thank God that believers of this church dispensation have already experienced many of the spiritual blessings of the New Covenant, which Israel nationally will not receive until a future day. That day is previewed in the next section.

THE SUFFERING SERVANT OF THE LORD (52:13—53:12)

Chapter 53, one of the best known chapters in the Word of God, is the middle chapter of the second section and therefore, the middle chapter of the whole second part of Isaiah. Its position is certainly not accidental. It gives a wonderful prophetic picture of the Lord Jesus Christ. The general theme of the second part of Isaiah (chaps. 40-66) is "The Comfort of God." The theme of this second section (chaps. 49-57) is "The Suffering Servant as the Redeemer." This chapter, the fourth of the Servant passages pertaining to the Messiah, reveals in greater measure than any other portion of the book the suffering of the Servant.

One should remember that in Isaiah the nation of Israel is sometimes the servant and Christ is sometimes the Servant. Although ancient Jewish scholars regarded the passage as messianic, many modern ones—unwilling to see the prophecy fulfilled in Jesus of Nazareth—take the suffering servant to be Israel.

The proofs that the chapter refers to the Lord Jesus Christ are many and varied. That aspect needs to be reviewed once more. The usage of the term *Servant of Yahweh* in Isaiah sometimes refers to Israel and sometimes to the Messiah. The one portrayed in this chapter is definitely the Servant of Yahweh (note 52:13 and 53:11), and therefore must be either Israel or the Messiah. It is not correct to bring in some other individual or group, such as Jeremiah or the prophets generally. That would be completely contrary to Isaiah's usage.

Which is it then? Is it not clear that the Servant in this passage is an individual and not a group? Furthermore, there are people speaking in the passage about the Servant. Those who are speaking are Israel, as will be shown. Consequently, the Servant must be the Messiah as in chapters 42 and 49.

Comparison with other prophetic passages shows that this passage is messianic. From Genesis 3:15 on, God in His Word traces the line of descent of the Redeemer and keeps adding details concerning Him. Some passages that can be compared with this one are Psalm 22 (the "psalm of the cross"); Psalm 69; Daniel 9:16; Zechariah 9:9; 12:10; and 13:7. It may also be added that this chapter is the climax to similar chapters in the book of Isaiah itself (42:4; 49:4; 50:6).

The description of what the Servant does simply does not fit Israel or any other entity or person other than Jesus Christ. The whole portrayal is that of a person. Moreover, it could never be said that God laid the iniquity of all men on the nation of Israel (53:6).

There is a consistent, uniform tradition about this chapter. The ancient Jews, before the coming of the Lord Jesus, took the passage as messianic. Ryrie mentions that the view of Israel as the suffering Servant did not arise until the twelfth century, although it has since become the leading interpretation among Jewish scholars.[6] In addition to the ancient Jewish tradition is the tradition of the early church and of the church generally, with the exception of modern rationalistic interpreters.

Add to those lines of evidence the negative one that no other satisfactory interpretation has ever been advanced. Those who deny a messianic interpretation cannot agree on any other meaning.

A person approaching the passage without previous indoctrina-

6. Ryrie, p. 1092.

tion could not help but see the similarity between what is said of the Servant of Yahweh in Isaiah 53 and what is seen of the Lord Jesus Christ in the Gospels. The prophecy and the history fit perfectly. The Servant is misunderstood and rejected; He suffers and dies. His sufferings are vicarious, voluntarily assumed, borne without complaint, and result in a glorious reward. Although the prophets emphasize the glory of the Messiah, He is also predicted as One who would suffer (cf. Gen. 3:15; Pss. 22 and 69; Dan. 9:26; Zech. 9:9; 12:10; 13:7). Furthermore, the expressions "tender shoot" and "root out of parched ground" strongly resemble titles used elsewhere of the Messiah (cf. 11:1; Zech. 3:8).

All of those evidences, weighty as they are, are overshadowed for a Christian by the weightier one that the New Testament expressly labels this as a prophecy about the Lord Jesus Christ. A large proportion of the references to the book of Isaiah, direct or indirect, in the New Testament are references to this chapter.

When Philip the deacon and evangelist met the Ethiopian treasurer on the deserted road to Gaza, the official asked him concerning this very chapter, "Please tell me, of whom does the prophet say this? Of himself, or of someone else?" (Acts 8:34) Philip had no uncertainty or hesitation. He answered immediately and unequivocally that it referred to Jesus Christ: "And Philip opened his mouth, and beginning from this Scripture he preached Jesus to him" (v. 35).

That is by no means the only quotation of this chapter in the New Testament. There are at least six direct quotations and a number of other allusions. The direct quotations are as follows:

52:15 is quoted in Romans 15:21
53:1 is quoted in John 12:38 and Romans 10:16
53:4 is quoted in Matthew 8:17
53:5-6 is quoted in 1 Peter 2:22-25
53:7-8 is quoted in Acts 8:32-33
53:12 is quoted in Mark 15:28 and Luke 22:37

Considering allusions to the language of Isaiah 53, here are some comparisons that show the wide influence of the chapter:

53:5 with Romans 4:25
53:7 with 1 Peter 1:19; Revelation 5:6 and 7:14
53:7 and 11 with John 1:29, 36
53:9 and 11 with 1 John 3:5
53:8-11 with 1 Corinthians 15:3, 4
53:8-11 with 2 Corinthians 5:21

Delitzsch, commenting on this chapter, said:

All the references in the New Testament to the Lamb of God (with which the corresponding allusions to the Passover are interwoven) spring from this passage in the Book of Isaiah. . . . The dumb type of the Passover now finds a tongue.[7]

The passage, which really begins with 52:13, is in five stanzas or strophes, each containing three verses. Some ancient Hebrew scholars have compared the strophes to the books of the Pentateuch:

1.	52:13-15	Genesis	The "seed-plot"
2.	53:1-3	Exodus	Redemption completed
3.	53:4-6	Leviticus	The offerings
4.	53:7-9	Numbers	The testings of earth
5.	53:10-12	Deuteronomy	Summary, with the desert journey past

Isaiah 53 has been called the "holy of holies" of Isaiah. The early church writer Polycarp spoke of it as the "golden passional" of the Old Testament. It is a great connecting link between Psalm 22 (psalm of the cross) and Psalm 110 (Christ's royal priesthood). It seems likely that all five of the major Levitical offerings are referred to in the chapter, for the Lord Jesus is the fulfillment of them all.

Keeping as closely as possible to the wording of the passage itself, we can outline it in this way:

7. Delitzsch, 2:323.

THE SUFFERING SERVANT OF THE LORD (52:13—53:12)

1. The Servant Exalted (52:13-15)
2. The Servant Despised (53:1-3)
3. The Servant Pierced (53:4-6)
4. The Servant Cut Off (53:7-9)
5. The Servant Satisfied (53:10-12)

THE FIRST STROPHE (52:13-15)

This first strophe gives a summary of the whole prophecy. At the beginning the Lord calls on men to look on His Servant (v. 13). This verse gazes on beyond the Messiah's suffering to the glorious exaltation, also described in Philippians 2:8-11. The suffering, however, must come first (v. 14).

How can one read about the torture inflicted on the "holy, harmless, undefiled" (Heb. 7:26, KJV) Son of God and Son of Man without being moved? Such torture, as described in Matthew 26:67-68 and 27:27-30, was to bring actual disfigurement to His countenance, such disfigurement as to cause great amazement. The suffering marvelously becomes the pathway to glory. Astonishment at His disfigurement is turned into wonder at His grace (v. 15).

Some commentators follow the reading "startle" instead of "sprinkle" at the beginning of verse 15. Alexander discusses this fully and comments:

> The real motive of the strange unanimity with which the true sense has been set aside, is the desire to obliterate this clear description, at the very outset, of the Servant of Jehovah as an expiatory purifier, one who must be innocent himself in order to cleanse others,—an office and a character alike inapplicable either to the prophets as a class, or to Israel as a nation, or even to the better class of Jews, much more to any single individual except to One who claimed to be the Purifier of the guilty, and to whom many nations do at this day ascribe whatever purity of heart or life they either have or hope for.[8]

As is often the case in Isaiah, the salvation brought by the suffering Servant is extended to the Gentiles as well as to the

8. Alexander, 2:288.

people of Israel. The "many nations" (v. 15) cannot be taken otherwise. How wonderful that God has put this exalted experience first to reassure His people that there is no doubt about the outcome of His Servant's suffering! The vicarious atonement was not to be in vain. With the final result in clear view the devout believer can understand something of God's infinite purpose.

THE SECOND STROPHE (53:1-3)

Some Hebrew scholars regard this prophecy as involving Israel, but they have cast Israel in the wrong role. Israel is indeed in the prophecy, but the suffering Servant is not Israel; the wondering speakers are. This is a prophetic picture of Israel's astonishment and remorse in the future national Day of Atonement (see Zech. 12:10) when national Israel will at last recognize the Lord Jesus as the Messiah.

This is the prophetic presentation of their thoughts at that time. They have difficulty immediately comprehending the reality of the Messiah. Who would have believed it, they ask, that this "tender shoot," this "root out of parched ground," this undesired One, this "despised and forsaken" One is really the Messiah after all?

There is difference of opinion about whether the expression *our message* (NASB) or *our report* (KJV) means "the report that we have given" or "the report that has come to us." It appears that the prophet is speaking as a representative of his enlightened people, and that he means the report that he had proclaimed. The expression "the arm of the LORD" impresses on the reader the almighty power of God in bringing about salvation through His suffering Servant.

In that exclamatory question the people admit their former unbelief.

The lowliness of the Lord Jesus is described next (v. 2). Although there is reason to believe from other passages of Scripture that the winsome character of the Lord Jesus appealed even to some of the most hopeless of men, this prophecy makes clear what some Christians do not fully comprehend—that the Lord Jesus Christ did not appear in such a way as to attract the natural man. Although the power of His deity was always present and was evident on occasion, there was no mere glamor about Him. He lived His earthly life in humble circumstances, not in worldly pomp. The natural mind is all too ready to construe meekness as weakness and to waste its adulation on the proud and self-seeking. "No beauty that we should desire him" (KJV) is the contemptuous but almost universal verdict, except of those whom the Father in His grace drew toward His beloved Son (John 6:44). It seems inconceivable to some that the Lord Jesus should be so despised. Here and there were the comparatively few disciples, the godly women who ministered to His material needs (Luke 8:2-3), the Roman centurion (Matt. 8:5-13), the Syrophoenician woman (Mark 7:25-30), and others. But the great mass was ready to cry out, "Crucify Him, crucify Him!"

Many who followed Him and thronged about Him in His ministry were only eager to see some exciting miracle or to eat of the supernaturally provided bread (John 6:26). It is also true today as well. Many who prate at length of the "lowly Nazarene" as a great teacher and good man speak only in hollow mockery. When the issue is joined, when the truths of the gospel are considered, when His deity and substitutionary atonement are in question, then they too despise and reject Him. Who can estimate the guilt of a self-righteous religious leader who sneers at the precious blood of Christ?

There is an important lesson here for believers. We should not seek the approval of a world that despises our Lord or desire acceptance by men who reject Him.

That was Israel's attitude toward the Savior. An almost exact parallel is drawn in the prologue to John's gospel: "He was in the world, and the world was made through Him, and the world did not know Him. He came to His own, and those who were His own did not receive Him" (John 1:10-11). We may thank God that many have received Him, called out from among the nations as a "people for His name" (Acts 15:14). This prophecy assures that Israel will eventually come to an acceptance of Him. They will look on Him whom "they have pierced" (Zech. 12:10). At that time of national repentance they will be sorry for their rejection of Him and will turn to Him in true repentance and faith.

THE THIRD STROPHE (53:4-6)

Verse 4 is one of the most controversial verses in the entire chapter. Because the word *griefs* means also "sicknesses," there are many who say that bodily healing is in the atonement, that a Christian does not need to be ill, and that illness is often if not invariably from lack of faith.

The whole tenor of the passage has to do with sin. Of course, its consequences have been and will be dealt with. Bodily infirmity is one of the consequences of Adam's sin visited on the whole human race, but the time for the removal of all physical illnesses has not yet arrived. In the context, the emphasis is on the spiritual "sickness" of sin.

The use made of this verse in the New Testament is instructive. The fulfillment is seen partially in the Lord Jesus Christ's sympathetically entering into the griefs and sorrows of people. Matthew 8:17 is explicit about that; it makes no reference to the substitutionary atonement of Christ, which is clearly in view in Isaiah 53:5-6.

The Lord Jesus had compassion on people during His earthly ministry, and healed a great many of them of their physical ailments. But not everyone during the Lord's stay on earth was healed and not all Christians are healed today. Paul had a "thorn in the flesh" that the Lord did not remove (2 Cor. 12:7-10). On one occasion Paul left Trophimus "sick at Miletus" (2 Tim. 4:20). On another occasion he wrote of Timothy's frequent illness (1 Tim. 5:23).

The time indeed is coming when the whole creation will be delivered from the bondage of corruption (Rom. 8:21). But that is not what people usually mean when they speak of healing in the atonement.

In this strophe, the believing remnant of Israel continues their musings. Although they, along with so many others, thought the suffering One suffered deservedly, in the future day they will realize that all of what He endured was vicarious—"our griefs He Himself bore" has the emphasis on *our*. What they had considered punishment for His blasphemy was instead His substitution for their own guilt (and ours).

The adversative at the beginning of verse 5 draws the contrast between what they had formerly believed about Him and what they now perceived. It was not for Himself, but for us! The verb translated "wounded" in the King James Version is literally "pierced through," as in the *New American Standard Bible*. It was obviously much more than a wound; it was a violent death.

Here is substitution in the exact sense of the term. Israel in Christ's day thought He deserved to die. He was accused of and condemned for blasphemy. He was considered deservedly smitten of God. Nevertheless, He died not for Himself but for others, and this prophecy is the assurance that Israel someday will realize this blessed truth. That is the heart of the wonderfully symmetrical second part of Isaiah. There is no higher truth than this: that the sinless Son of God died on the cross for sinful man. One can fully understand why Isaiah is called the prophet of the gospel.

Not only was the divine Substitute "pierced through," but He was "crushed for our iniquities" (v. 5). Here is a Hebrew word that means "crushed," "broken," or "smitten." Compare the prophecy in Genesis 3:15 where a synonym is used.

One day the Lord Jesus looked compassionately on the multitudes of Israel who were "like sheep without a shepherd" (Matt. 9:36); "each . . . to his own way" (Isa. 53:6). That is what men want. They think they are free and working out their own destiny; instead, they are lost.

God in His infinite grace provided salvation for the wandering sheep. "Christ died for our sins" (1 Cor. 15:3). The expression *caused . . . to fall on Him* means literally "to cause to strike with great force," or "with terrific impact." Paul explains it in these words: "He made Him who knew no sin to be sin on our behalf, that we might become the righteousness of God in Him" (2 Cor. 5:21).

Peter, under the inspiration of the Holy Spirit, refers to this passage, reminding believers that they have a Shepherd who is also the overseer of their souls (1 Peter 2:25). It is significant that in this same passage Christ is seen both as the sacrificial Lamb and as the Shepherd of the sheep. That is the culmination of a number of Old Testament passages in which God is seen as the Shepherd of His people (see Pss. 23:1 and 80:1). In the New Testament the Lord Jesus unhesitatingly refers those passages to Himself in His claim to be "the good shepherd" who "lays down His life for the sheep" (John 10:11). He is also the Great Shepherd, risen from the dead (Heb. 13:20-21) and the Chief Shepherd, who is coming again (1 Pet. 5:4). Hence, He is seen in His past, present, and future ministries.

THE FOURTH STROPHE (53:7-9)

The next strophe, speaking of the Servant cut off, is a reminder of the gentleness and patience of the Lord Jesus as the sacrifice. He was not an unwilling victim compelled to go to the cross. He said to those opposing Him: "No one takes it from Me, but I lay it down of Myself. I have power to lay it down, and I have power to take it again" (John 10:18, NKJV). He also said solemnly to Pontius Pilate, "You would have no authority over Me, unless it had been given you from above" (John 19:11).

He was indeed the voluntary sacrifice. The path from glory to Calvary was illuminated by His "Lo, I come . . . to do thy will, O God" (Heb. 10:7, KJV). Here indeed, as Delitzsch so aptly said, the Passover "finds a tongue." All through the centuries since Moses' time the Passover lambs had been killed, all pointing forward to Someone, yet giving only a silent and cryptic witness. Now, that Someone is revealed and the sequence is perfectly clear. It is but a step from Isaiah 53:7 to John 1:29, for John the Baptist announced: "Behold, the Lamb of God who takes away the sin of the world!"

In regard to the silence of the Lord Jesus before His accusers one should consult Matthew 26:63-64. This is further elaborated by Peter: "And while being reviled, He did not revile in return; while suffering, He uttered no threats, but kept entrusting Himself to Him who judges righteously" (1 Pet. 2:23). It was not that He did not speak at all, for He did testify to His deity when the high priest flatly asked Him, "Are You the Christ, the Son of the Blessed One?" (Mark 14:61). He replied plainly, "I am" (Mark 14:62). The point of the prophecy is that there was no complaint from mankind's perfect substitute. He did not open His mouth to complain or repine. He willingly accepted the judgment from His heavenly Father.

The prophecy proceeds to the thoughtlessness of His generation. "He was cut off out of the land of the living"; condemned by His own people, yet graciously bearing their transgressions. Daniel was likewise to speak later of the cutting off of the Messiah (Dan. 9:26). With what seemingly irrelevant details prophecy is sometimes concerned! Yet that which appears to be irrelevant furnishes proof of the genuineness of the prophecy. There could be no accidental fulfillment of such a prediction as this. He who was crucified between two evildoers was buried in the tomb of a rich man, Joseph of Arimathaea (Matt. 27:57).

THE FIFTH STROPHE (53:10-12)

Men see the death of the Lord Jesus Christ only as a tragedy. They imagine a visionary martyr, perhaps ahead of His time, suffering and dying for His ideals. Such an interpretation of

Christ's death is a travesty. God's Word shows that what in one sense is a tragedy is also the source of the deepest joy.

What Christ suffered at the hands of men was tragic. They took Him and with "wicked hands" crucified and killed Him, as Peter declared (Acts 2:23, KJV). Nevertheless, in and through that tragedy God was working out His sovereign purpose of grace. Isaiah emphasizes that in verse 10.

The most mysterious and glorious fact about the death of Christ is that He was God's sacrificial Lamb. In a way that we cannot comprehend, He took our place in bearing the righteous judgment of God against sin. That was the depth of the suffering of the Lord Jesus, which caused Him to cry out in the thick supernatural darkness, "My God, My God, why hast Thou forsaken Me?" (Matt. 27:46).

It was from that suffering that His holy soul shrank in the Garden of Gethsemane—not from fear, but from its very holiness. Many brave people have borne great physical and mental suffering unflinchingly, but only the sinless Son of God could endure such suffering. To be made sin—how little any person can know of the effect that would have in the soul of One who is perfectly sinless!

But the Lord Jesus could look beyond the suffering. "Who for the joy set before Him," that is, in exchange for that He "endured the cross, despising the shame, and has sat down at the right hand of the throne of God" (Heb. 12:2). "He will see His offspring," (v. 10). The Lord Jesus had in view that great multitude of sons whom He was to bring into glory (Heb. 2:10). When viewed in this light the death of Christ is not a tragedy or a waste, but the greatest triumph possible. That is proved by the fact that death could not hold Him: "He will prolong His days" (v. 10). The Old Testament in a number of passages foresees the resurrection of Christ, that other essential element of the gospel along with His substitutionary death (1 Cor. 15:3-4).

"He will see it and be satisfied" (v. 11). How many times in human history men have dared to accomplish stupendous feats all for nothing! Not so with the Lord Jesus. Here is the crown of His atonement—"satisfied." The question facing every individual who comes in contact with that truth is, Are you satisfied? To put it even more personally, Am I satisfied with what the Lord Jesus has done for me on the cross? By the knowledge of Himself, God's righteous Servant justifies us. He can do that because He already has borne our iniquities. "By him all that believe," the Scripture says, "are justified from all things" (Acts 13:39, KJV).

The prophecy closes with the same thought with which it began—exaltation after the suffering. In this brief passage are seen both of the major themes of Old Testament prophecy: "The sufferings of Christ and the glories to follow" (1 Pet. 1:11). The spoils of this tremendous and unique campaign are now divided. The Messiah has come into His own. Psalms 2 and 72 are good examples of other prophetic Scriptures speaking of the coming day of Christ's triumph and millennial reign.

It is possible to read a passage such as Isaiah 53 and see it only as a dim and far-off event, something that had meaning to the prophet and the people of Isaiah's time but not to those of the present day, because "the god of this world has blinded the minds of the unbelieving, that they might not see the light of the gospel of the glory of Christ, who is the image of God" (2 Cor. 4:4).

To the seeking heart, the believing heart, the Lord Jesus is revealed in all the sad-joyous tragedy-triumph of His substitution-ary, sacrificial death and in all the unalloyed joy and triumph of His glorious bodily resurrection. The Servant of the Lord (Yah-weh) is the Christ of Calvary and the empty tomb.

RESTORATION OF ISRAEL TO THE PLACE OF BLESSING (54:1-17)

The chapters that follow (54-57) describe the salvation that the Servant has provided through His vicarious death. One should not lose sight of that relationship. The redemption accomplished in chapter 53 is now applied to the nation of Israel and to the individual believer. Because Israel is not specifically mentioned by name in chapter 54, some commentators gratuitously read into it the church as though it and Israel were identical.

Isaiah tells of the comfort of God for Israel, but that comfort is extended by God's grace to the whole world. Christians can be thankful that through faith in the Lord Jesus Christ every believer, whether Jew or Gentile, can now enter into the spiritual benefits of His death. However, that does not alter the fact that God has made national promises to Israel that He has not made to any other nation.

In chapter 54 the nation is seen as a barren, desolate wife restored to fellowship and blessing. One can readily see the figurative language in a passage such as this. Israel is more than once compared to a wife. The interpretative principle that must be insisted on is that figurative language does not change the overall literal fulfillment of prophecy. The most basic principle of Bible interpretation is at stake, and those who deny any future blessings for the nation of Israel have cast themselves adrift on a hopeless sea of allegorism, without chart or compass.

There is a partial fulfillment in the return of the people from the Babylonian captivity and their reinhabiting of cities that had been in ruins, but the complete fulfillment will occur in the millennium. To view this as a missionary passage and see in it the present spread of the gospel throughout the earth is contrary to the New Testament pattern.

Young points out that Isaiah does not make as much use of the figure of the marriage relationship as do Jeremiah and Hosea. Hosea narrates the poignant story of his own wife's unfaithfulness, desertion, and eventual restoration as an analogy to the unfaithful nation of Israel leaving her Husband. The coming back is stressed here in this passage of Isaiah.

Israel's dwelling is compared to a tent that is being enlarged (v. 2), perhaps looking back to the manner of life of Abraham and his immediate descendants—the tent signifying their pilgrim character on the earth.

Many Gentiles will undoubtedly be surprised and chagrined to find that Israel is to have the leading place among the nations of the world (v. 3). God has a relationship to Israel that He has never had and never will have to any other nation—"thy Maker is thine husband" (v. 5, KJV). His name is stressed: Yahweh of hosts (no doubt a reference to the heavenly armies, as in Luke 2:13). The *New International Version* seems somewhat bland and inexact in consistently translating *Yahweh* of hosts as LORD Almighty, thereby losing the nuances of the original.

Further emphasis is placed on the Lord as the Redeemer, and then Isaiah's characteristic expression is used—"the Holy One of Israel." How wonderful to be assured that this great God who has this special relationship by covenant with Israel is also "the God of all the earth" (v. 5).

Paul speaks of that in his consideration of the place of Israel in God's purpose:

I say then, they did not stumble so as to fall, did they? May it never be! But by their transgression salvation has come to the Gentiles, to make them jealous. Now if their transgression be riches for the world and their failure be riches for the Gentiles, how much more will their fulfillment be! . . . For if their rejection be the reconciliation of the world, what will their acceptance be but life from the dead? [Rom. 11:11-12, 15]

That passage from Isaiah, as well as many others, speaks of the "acceptance" ("receiving," KJV) of Israel, its restoration to the place of blessing in the earth. It cannot help but affect the nations and the whole world.

God's severe judgment on Israel is viewed as but "for a brief moment" (v. 7) in comparison to the glory that is to come. The "moment" in which He hid His face from them is contrasted with the "everlasting lovingkindness" (v. 8) that He will manifest to them in the future. God reminds them of His promise to Noah that the earth would never again be destroyed by a flood (v. 9), and draws a parallel that once His judgment has been executed on faithless Israel He will restore her and will not repeat the judgment. In regard to verses 11-17 Ryrie comments, "The full accomplishment of what is described here for Israel awaits the millennial age."[9]

Israel's situation as described in the closing verses of the chapter is like that of all justified people in all ages: "Every tongue that accuses you in judgment you will condemn" and "their vindication is from Me" (v. 17). As Paul exclaims concerning the saved:

Who will bring a charge against God's elect? God is the one who justifies; who is the one who condemns? Christ Jesus is He who died, yes, rather who was raised, who is at the right hand of God, who also intercedes for us. [Rom. 8:33-34]

APPEAL TO COME TO GOD FOR SALVATION (55:1-13)

This section of nine chapters (49-57) has as its major theme "The Suffering Servant as the Redeemer." As has been seen, the heart of the section is chapter 53. The chapters following that climactic provision of redemption show its application, first to Israel (54:1-17) and then in the appeal going out to all the world (55:1-13).

God's Word is filled with such gracious appeals. The only requisite for coming to Him is a burning thirst (cf. John 7:37 and

9. Ryrie, p. 1095.

Rev. 22:17). This is no ordinary thirst, but rather the "hunger and thirst for righteousness" of which the Lord Jesus spoke (Matt. 5:6).

In this context the appeal is addressed primarily to Israel, but in its application it is as broad as the human race. Everyone who seeks the Lord in the manner described here will surely find Him.

The appeal stresses the fact that God's salvation cannot be bought. It must be received only as a free gift of God's grace. "By grace . . . through faith . . . not of works" (Eph. 2:8-9, KJV). "The gift of God is eternal life through Jesus Christ our Lord" (Rom. 6:23, KJV).

The individual who (ignorant of God's free gift) is seeking to earn or pay for that which can never satisfy, is brought up short by the admonition of the Lord: "Why do you spend money for what is not bread, and your wages for what does not satisfy? . . . Listen carefully to Me . . . Incline your ear and come to Me" (vv. 2-3). God promises an everlasting covenant (v. 3), undoubtedly a reference to the "new covenant" announced in Jeremiah 31:31 and referred to in the New Testament by the Lord Jesus as well as by the writer to the Hebrews (Heb. 10:16-18). The "sure mercies of David" (v. 3, KJV) are evidently the "faithful mercies shown to David" (NASB).

F. C. Jennings, after quoting Acts 13:32-34 where Paul in the synagogue at Antioch in Pisidia refers to this passage on the "sure mercies of David," says this:

> Do we not see that no "mercy" could be made "sure" for poor sinning Jews, still less such poor sinners of the Gentiles as you and I are, my fellow-sinner—my fellow-saint—except in our sins being forever put away in sternest justice; and they have—*they have!* "He was delivered for our offenses, and was raised for our justification": and high above principalities and powers, He sits, whose sacred Head was weighted with our sins. . . . Verses 4 and 5 tell us that those mercies go far beyond Israel, for "He is not the God of the Jews only, but of the Gentiles also."[10]

Jennings goes on to say that some do not regard this as a gospel-call, since it is God who seeks man. But God seeks men by leading them to seek Him (see John 6:37, 45). As an anonymous hymn writer said:

10. F.C. Jennings, *Studies in Isaiah*, p. 647.

> I sought the Lord, and afterward I knew
> He moved my soul to seek Him, seeking me;
> It was not I that found, O Savior true;
> No, I was found of Thee.

The seeking of the Lord (v. 6) is connected with the idea that God is infinite, that His thoughts and ways are utterly different from those of sinful man (v. 8). The Lord Jesus promised that the one who drank of the water He gave should never thirst again (John 4:14). This whole passage is founded on the solemn declaration of God. Is there any doubt that His Word will be fulfilled? None whatever is His own assurance: "My word . . . shall not return to Me empty" (v. 11). All the glorious prophecies of blessings flowing from the suffering of the Servant will be fulfilled.

The chapter closes with a poetic description of millennial joy. Nature is seen as celebrating the glories of its Creator. There is an intimation in Romans and elsewhere of the wonder of the creation when it is freed from the Adamic curse. The millennial earth will be indescribably more wonderful than the present earth—the same planet but renewed and glorified by the power of Almighty God, and with His reversal of the judgment brought on it after Adam sinned.

Those who deny, reject, or slight the millennium are leaving out a very important part of God's redemptive program. It is essential that God be glorified here on earth in the same locale in which He has been disobeyed and rejected. The Lord Jesus Christ, who suffered and died on this planet, must reign over it. The millennial joy of the chapter may be compared with the song of salvation in chapter 12 and with some of the millennial psalms, such as 46, 72, and 98.

MORAL EXHORTATIONS IN VIEW OF GOD'S SALVATION (56:1-12)

Salvation always brings with it the obligation of godly living. Because God's salvation is about to come, His people need to be prepared for it spiritually. This righteousness is described here in an Old Testament setting of Sabbath-keeping, but the eternal principle is not hard to find. It is the principle of trust in God and obedience to Him (vv. 1-2). True worship, even in the Old Testament economy of ceremony and symbol, was in reality a matter of the heart.

The mention of the "foreigner" (vv. 3, 6) shows that the blessings of the millennial kingdom will be extended to the Gentiles. Christ's reign will be worldwide. In the face of many passages that stress it, it seems strange that so many interpreters completely evade the issue. Generally, the reason seems to lie in a nonliteral hermeneutic and theology that does not acknowledge dispensational distinctions. If people would simply accept the truisms that Israel is Israel, the Gentiles are the Gentiles, and the church is the church, many exegetical problems could be avoided.

God's special concern for the eunuchs, who could not have a natural posterity and who were excluded under the law from the congregation (Deut. 23:1), is expressed in verses 3-5. "An everlasting name which will not be cut off" is not just an eternal remembrance of those people by others but signifies their personal eternal life.

The calling of the Gentiles ("the foreigners," v. 6) in that future day again strikes the note of universality (not universalism, for not all will be saved). It is reassuring to know that people of all nations will be gathered together in our blessed Lord's millennial kingdom to worship in the Temple, which is primarily a "house of prayer" (v. 7). The Lord Jesus quoted from this verse when He cleansed the Temple: "And He said to them, 'It is written, "My house shall be called a house of prayer"; but you are making it a robbers' den'" (Matt. 21:13; cf. Mark 11:17; Luke 19:46).

A contrast is made in the closing verses of this chapter (vv. 9-12) between the believing ones previously described and the false prophets, who are called blind watchmen and "dumb dogs unable to bark." Thinking only of their personal gain (material, not spiritual), they are "shepherds who have no understanding" (v. 11). A number of times in Scripture the people of God are compared to sheep and their leaders to shepherds. The example of the shepherd who fleeces the flock instead of feeding the flock is well attested. Just as the sheep have turned to their own way (53:6), so too the shepherds "have all turned to their own way" (56:11).

CONTRAST OF THE CONTRITE AND THE WICKED (57:1-21)

When God's salvation is made known to men, there are always those who accept it and those who reject it. There were those in Isaiah's day and afterward who would not be warned concerning the judgment that was to come in the captivity. They could not or would not understand that the righteous man who died was being "taken away from the evil to come" (v. 1, KJV).

The description of sins and follies is horrible in its forthrightness, including sex orgies and the slaughter of infants in sacrifice (v. 5). Jennings observes:

> Under such repellent terms is simple departure of heart from the Lord pictured. Oh, how little is thought of that among men! No laws are aimed at it; no court takes notice of it; Society is very lenient to such violators; but well may we be sure, and lay it to heart, that the same unfaithfulness on the part of our God's present "witness," the professing Church, is not looked at with any greater complacency this very day.
>
> Let us not think for a moment that "our God" who is also "a consuming fire," can endure complacently in Christendom what He so abhorred in Israel, nor that greater privilege diminishes responsibility; it vastly enhances it.[11]

The contrite and lowly of spirit are in sharp antithesis to the apostate portion of the nation just described. God is preparing the way for the former by preparing for their restoration and eventual millennial glory.

Isaiah contains passages of transcendent beauty concerning the personality and majesty of the Lord. They are transcendently beautiful because they are true and present God in His condescending grace. Although He is "the high and exalted One who lives forever, whose name is Holy" (v. 15), He is willing to live with "the contrite and lowly of spirit."

Earthly sovereigns are thought of as dwelling with the exalted and proud; the great Sovereign of all dwells with the humble believer. That is a consolation and an encouragement to the trusting heart. However, there is danger that the believer will fasten his thoughts on himself rather than on God and as a result lose his humility. A real view of God, such as Isaiah has described from his own experience in chapter 6, will provoke contrition and humility.

The pronouncement of peace to the far and the near (v. 19) sounds parallel to the teaching in Ephesians concerning the fact that the Lord Jesus Christ *is* peace, *made* peace, and came and *preached* peace to the near (Israel) and the far (the Gentiles), and

11. Ibid., p. 664.

"broke down the barrier of the dividing wall" (Eph. 2:14, cf. vv. 11-22).

The contrast to the contrite is described in the concluding verses (20-21). This refrain echoes the one at the end of chapter 48, and in both instances marks off a sectional division.

One might almost think that God is describing the present day. Certainly there is increasing restlessness abroad in the world. People run here and there seeking satisfaction in this or that, trying this panacea and that nostrum, but remaining without peace and rest. One does not have to be a vile criminal in the eyes of men to fall into the classification described here. The contrast is between the contrite and the wicked, between the repentant forgiven sinner and the unrepentant, unforgiven sinner. A person is either one or the other. The New Testament shows that rejection of the Lord Jesus Christ is the most heinous and reprehensible of all sins:

He who believes in Him is not judged; he who does not believe has been judged already, because he has not believed in the name of the only begotten Son of God. [John 3:18]

He who believes in the Son has eternal life; but he who does not obey the Son shall not see life, but the wrath of God abides on him. [v. 36]

True peace of any kind can come only through the Lord Jesus Christ, the Redeemer, who has been prophetically described in this section as the suffering Servant of Yahweh. The section closes with the refrain, echoed from 48:22: " 'There is no peace,' says my God, 'for the wicked.' "

10

The Glorious Consummation

(58:1—66:24)

This is the last of the three sections in the second part of Isaiah. Note the structure of these concluding nine chapters in the setting of the division and the whole book.

ISAIAH—THE SALVATION OF THE LORD

PART ONE: THE JUDGMENT OF GOD UPON ISRAEL (1-39)
PART TWO: THE COMFORT OF GOD FOR ISRAEL (40-66)
I. Deliverance of God's People (40-48)
II. The Suffering Servant as the Redeemer (49-57)
III. The Glorious Consummation (58:1—66:24)
   A. Repentance Followed by Blessing (58:1-14)
   B. The Coming of the Redeemer to Zion (59:1-21)
   C. The Glory of Israel (60:1-22)
   D. The Ministry of the Messiah (61:1-11)
   E. "Jerusalem a Praise in the Earth" (62:1-12)
   F. The Day of Vengeance (63:1-19)
   G. The Prayer of the Remnant (64:1-12)
   H. Condemnation and Glory (65:1-25)
   I. Peace Like a River (66:1-24)

REPENTANCE FOLLOWED BY BLESSING (58:1-14)

The closing section of the prophecy describes the glorious outcome that God has for Israel, the people of the Servant and God's channel of blessing to the world. There is a strong contrast throughout the section between the rebellious and the faithful, a contrast that is never entirely absent from any extended portion of the Word of God.

As at the very beginning of Isaiah, much of the worship of God by Israel was described as only formal or nominal at best and hypocritical and sinful at worst; so here the lesson is repeated that the outward forms of repentance do not necessarily indicate a change of heart. Fasting, unaccompanied by doing what is right, is not sufficient (v. 6). Practical righteousness is what God enjoins here (cf. James 1:25-26). The curse of Israel, and indeed of the church also, is outward conformity without inward transformation of life.

The Scripture gives assurance that when one fully trusts the Lord, He will give that metamorphosis (see Rom. 12:2) that is needed so desperately. Young's comment is appropriate and helpful:

> In the second half of the verse (3) the Lord states why He has not seen nor known their worship. They have combined worship with their own pleasure. On the day of their fast, when the heart should be directed in meditation toward God, they have found a time for their own *pleasure*.[1]

Participating in true worship will result in God's hearing and responding to their cry (v. 9). The setting alludes in some degree to the restoration of the land and the cities after the Babylonian captivity, but it undoubtedly also looks far ahead to millennial times. Delight in the Lord will cause His people to "ride on the heights of the earth" (v. 14) and to inherit what God has promised to the descendants of Jacob. The expression "For the mouth of the LORD has spoken" (v. 14) echoes the same declaration found in 1:20 and 40:5 and is one of the stylistic marks of Isaiah.

THE COMING OF THE REDEEMER TO ZION (59:1-21)

Chapter 59 continues in the same vein as the preceding chapter. What is it that causes the one who prays to feel that he is not heard? It is sin (v. 2). It is always true that the fault is not with God but with the one who calls on God. God is always ready to give the answer and to provide the deliverance. Paul makes somewhat extensive use of this chapter in Romans 3 in his summarization of the universal sinfulness of mankind apart from the grace of God.

1. Edward J. Young, *The Book of Isaiah* (NIC), 3:417.

After Israel's sins have been described, there is confession on the part of the remnant. Long after Isaiah's time (toward the close of the Babylonian captivity) Daniel prayed in this way, confessing the sins of the people, not as an outsider who was uninvolved but identifying himself with his people: "O Lord . . . we have sinned, committed iniquity, acted wickedly, and rebelled, even turning aside from Thy commandments and ordinances" (Dan. 9:4-5).

Since God could not find among the nation at this time those who could be true intercessors, He provided salvation in His sovereign grace and righteousness (v. 16). This leads to the same wonderful Person who has appeared in so many different ways in this incomparable prophecy of Isaiah—the Redeemer, the Lord Jesus Christ. At His first coming He provided salvation, but that salvation will not be applied to Israel nationally until He comes again—"A redeemer will come to Zion" (v. 20). The word *redeemer* is often used of a person who acts as a kinsman in taking care of his family. This Redeemer is related to mankind as has been intimated all through the prophecy; He is Immanuel (7:14). He is God, but He is also man.

THE GLORY OF ISRAEL (60:1-22)

Chapter 60 describes Israel's coming glory in the future messianic kingdom. The first three verses show the coming of the light. This exhortation is addressed to Jerusalem, which is seen as in deep darkness because of sin. It is reminiscent of chapter 9 and again speaks of the Messiah. Light and deliverance come through Him. As might be expected, there are also foreviews of the final fulfillment in intimations of the return from the Babylonian captivity. Paul uses the same sort of expression in 2 Corinthians 4:6 when he says: "For God, who said, 'Light shall shine out of darkness,' is the One who has shone in our hearts to give the light of the knowledge of the glory of God in the face of Christ." Delitzsch comments about the opening of this paragraph: "Zion lies prostrate on the ground, smitten down by the judgment of God, brought down to the ground by inward prostration and partly overcome by the sleep of self-security."[2] Jerusalem is to reflect the light that comes from the Lord (cf. Mal. 4:2).

2. Franz Delitzsch, *Biblical Commentary on the Prophecies of Isaiah*, 2:409.

Like the "Sun of righteousness" (Mal. 4:2, KJV) the Lord comes upon them as a rising sun, dispelling the "deep darkness" (Isa. 60:2) of sin and ignorance, a worldwide darkness. Israel in the kingdom age will fulfill the role God intended for her—to be the channel of His blessing to the whole world. From verse 3 some have inferred that the magi mentioned in Matthew 2 were kings, but the verse is not applicable to that event at the Lord's first coming; it is rather a reference to the salvation of the nations in the last days through restored Israel.

The mention of the glory of the Lord (v. 2) carries one back in thought to chapter 40 where also it was mentioned that "the glory of the LORD will be revealed" (v. 5). In this place there is the added thought that the light that falls on Israel will attract the Gentiles. The exhortation to Zion in verse 4 is to lift up her eyes and turn them in all directions, for "she is the object sought by an approaching multitude."[3]

The chapter describes in some detail the homage that the Gentiles will pay to Israel. God's righteousness requires just retribution for the mistreatment accorded Israel in the past by many nations. Those who are in bondage to the terrible bias of anti-Semitism will not like what God says here.

You will "be radiant," God says (v. 5; cf. Ps. 34:6). The abundance described is probably of both persons and things. Sheba (v. 6) is in southern Arabia and is noted as a source of gold. Kedar and Nebaioth were lands always rich in flocks and herds. A very vivid figure is used, as the sacrificial victims voluntarily give themselves up to sacrifice. Many commentators incorrectly put the church into the scene.

The figures at the beginning of verse 8 express swiftness. The answer to the question "Who are these?" is given in verse 9. It is a description of ships bringing back sons of Israel from distant places. It is as though the coastlands are waiting for the appointed signal from God. Tarshish can not be positively identified, but it is seen as a great maritime center. Many take it as a region in southern Spain (cf. Jonah 1:3). The great fleet brings Zion's children from afar and with them a great treasure.

3. Ibid., p. 411.

Gentiles will not only give their possessions, but will also be servants of Israel themselves in that glad day. Compare the thought of verse 11 with Zechariah 14:7 and Revelation 21:25. The Gentiles are led captive in a triumphal possession (v. 11; cf. 45:14). The welfare of the nations depends on their submission to Israel (v. 12; cf. Zech. 10:1; 14:16). "The glory of Lebanon" (v. 13) is its magnificent cedar trees, which apparently will be used in the building of the millennial Temple. The expression "the place of My feet" is in keeping with other passages where the Temple is called God's footstool (cf. Pss. 99:5; 132:7; Lam. 2:1; 1 Chron. 28:2). As mentioned before, many proud and arrogant Gentiles are and will be offended by this plain language spoken by God Himself. Israel, which in its sinful rebellion has become a laughingstock and byword to many nations, will in that future day be addressed by the honorable name of "the city of the LORD, the Zion of the Holy One of Israel" (v. 14).

The remainder of the chapter describes the glorified city. The prosperity of restored Israel is comparable to the days of Solomon, but far better because it will not be accompanied by injustice or discontent (see 1 Kings 1:27; 2 Chron. 9:20, 27). Some take the promise of verse 19 as one of prosperity expressed in figurative language. However, it seems to be more than that; it is a promise of the presence of God (cf. Ezek. 48:35 and Rev. 22). There seems to be here a blending of millennial conditions with the eternal state.

The Lord's promises are sure. He will bring to accomplishment what He has purposed. Astonishing changes are in store for this earth—moral, political, and economic changes. When God works His sovereign purpose as described in these prophecies, Israel will be a witness to Himself as He intended it. When Israel becomes what it is supposed to be and the Gentiles assume their appointed place in relation to Israel, then there will be righteousness and peace in the earth. All of that depends on a Person, the Person who speaks in the next chapter.

THE MINISTRY OF THE MESSIAH (61:1-11)

Chapters 61-63 form the heart of this concluding section of Isaiah's prophecy. In chapter 61 the Messiah's ministry is described; in chapter 62 the result of that ministry is seen in Israel's restoration; in chapter 63 the day of vengeance is announced and the prayer and praise of the believing remnant of the nation are given. In Isaiah, it is sometimes hard to know who is speaking. At the beginning of chapter 61 the speaker tells us that He has been anointed. That is the root from which the term *Messiah* ("the anointed One") comes. The word *anointed* is the clue, and the New Testament is the proof that the speaker here is none other than the Lord Jesus Christ.

In this passage there is again a blending together of the two advents of the Lord Jesus. The present age between the advents, the age in which we are living, is not the specific subject of Old Testament prophecy. In fact, Peter explains that the prophets themselves were perplexed about the seeming contradictions in the predictions concerning "the sufferings of Christ, and the glory that should follow" (1 Pet. 1:11, KJV). From observing that one can learn to look for the proper distinctions in prophecy. One also can see how fulfilled prophecies set the pattern for those yet unfulfilled.

This is the passage from which the Lord Jesus Himself read in the synagogue at Nazareth, as recorded in Luke 4:16-31. The way He did it and the statement He made about the prophecy ought to be conclusive proof that He Himself is the speaker in the passage. If one can cut through the murkiness of some of the commentaries that view this as only indirectly relating to Christ or through the outright darkness of those who refer it to the prophet Isaiah or the prophets generally—and that in the face of the New Testament evidence—one can then perceive the messianic picture. In His reading the Lord Jesus read only a part of the passage, stopping in the middle of a sentence. The reason for His stopping is obvious, for He followed His public reading of the Scripture by announcing, "Today this Scripture has been fulfilled in your hearing" (Luke 4:27). He had read only the part that was fulfilled that day; the remainder, having to do with the "day of vengeance of our God," was not being fulfilled at that time and will not be until the return of the Lord.

To leave out the future earthly kingdom, as amillennial commentators do, is to place prophecies such as this one in a kind of ethereal atmosphere in which one can see shadowy figures but can never come to grips with the realities of the situation. Ryrie comments:

The ministry of the Messiah at His first coming is described in verses 1-2a and at His second coming in verses 2b-3. In claiming to be Messiah, Jesus Christ read in the synagogue only that which applied to His ministry during His first coming (Luke 4:18-19).[4]

This is the natural and logical way to interpret the passage—that Luke, under the guidance of the Holy Spirit, not only records that the Lord Jesus read the passage from Isaiah, but that He read only the part that Luke records, and that there is as much significance in what He did not read as there is in what He read. Scripture in other places has more to say about the day of vengeance, as will be seen in connection with chapter 63.

The Messiah says, "The spirit of the Lord GOD [Adonai Yahweh] is upon Me" (v. 1). Here the three Persons of the Godhead are mentioned together in the same brief clause: the Lord GOD, His Spirit and the Speaker, the Messiah, or, in New Testament language, the Father, the Spirit, and the Son. In connection with Isaiah's commission (Isa. 6) it was shown that the Old Testament contains numerous intimations of the Trinity, although the full exposition of the doctrine is reserved for the New Testament. Progressive revelation is a reality, but not in the sense that liberal critics of the Bible suppose. There are no contradictions between later parts and earlier part; no correcting of previously recorded material. The progress is not from imperfection to perfection, for all the Word of God is perfect, but from incompleteness to completeness. Even without the New Testament, a careful reader of the passage could discern three personalities; the New Testament confirms Their identity.

Some of the great heroes of Old Testament times could say that the Spirit of God was on them for the tasks to which God had called them (e.g., Judg. 6:34), but none could say it in the same measure that this One could. The Lord Jesus Christ, the Son of God and Son of Man, is the One to whom the Holy Spirit has been given in all His infinite fullness, for there was never any hindrance of any kind in His life. His perfect humanity, completely subject to the will of the Father, is in view as well as His absolute deity. John says of Him: "For he whom God hath sent speaketh the words of God: for God giveth not the Spirit by measure unto him" (John 3:34, KJV).

4. Charles C. Ryrie, *The Ryrie Study Bible* (NASB), p. 1104.

The amazing Speaker in the synagogue at Nazareth went on reading the Isaianic passage: "Because the *Lord* has anointed me" (v. 1). At the baptism of the Lord Jesus the voice of God the Father came from heaven saying, "This is My beloved Son, in whom I am well-pleased" (Matt. 3:17), and the Holy Spirit descended in bodily form like a dove upon Him. He is the fulfiller of all the types (divinely appointed prophetic symbols) of anointing in the Old Testament—the anointing of prophets, of priests, and of kings. The application of oil to these officials was a symbol of their enduement of power by the Holy Spirit of God, equipping and enabling them for the offices into which they were being inducted.

As the Lord Jesus read those wonderful words from Isaiah's prophecy and began to comment on them, it is no wonder that "the eyes of all in the synagogue were fixed upon Him" (Luke 4:20). Here was something that could not happen often—a man was actually claiming to be the long-promised Messiah, so long prophesied and so long awaited. No doubt through the centuries others had made similar claims, but this Man was different. No one ever had or could have such credentials as He. There is no ambiguity here; there could be no misunderstanding of what He claimed. In fact, the New Testament is perfectly plain in describing how the religious leaders of His time were quite clear and quite right in their knowledge of what He claimed to be. For example, they said on one occasion that they wanted to condemn Him "for blasphemy; and because You, being a man, make Yourself out to be God" (John 10:33). In that respect they were much more intellectually honest than the humanistic, rationalistic theologians of today who allege that Jesus never claimed to be God. But they were mistaken in their response to Him and, as a result, stand utterly condemned in the light of His presence.

We can envision ourselves in a similar situation in our churches today. Suppose someone stood up in the assembly and said that he was the one referred to in an Old Testament prophecy that clearly implied deity. Would not this be an occasion for astonishment? Such an impostor would undoubtedly be ushered out!

There was something about this man in Nazareth's synagogue that distinguished Him from all imposters and misguided zealots. There was something about Him and His solemn claims that incited the admiration of even the most grudging critic: "And all were speaking well of Him, and wondering at the gracious words which were falling from His lips" (Luke 4:22).

Obviously He was no fanatic or wild-eyed dreamer, and just as obviously not a charlatan or pretender. There is no one who ever had the equanimity and poise of the Lord Jesus. His forthright assertions demanded attention. In view of that, one might think His words would have been received with joy and thanksgiving. Here was the hope of many centuries; the long-foretold Redeemer was in their very midst. He was announcing the fulfillment of Isaiah's prophecy and by implication the whole body of prophetic truth.

But as He went on, animosity and opposition manifested themselves and began to grow. Finally, the people of Nazareth rose up in sinful wrath against Him and actually tried to kill Him by casting Him over a precipice. The hill of the precipitation, pointed out in Nazareth today, remains a mute testimony (whether the presently accepted hill is the actual one or not) to the corruption of the human heart apart from the grace of God.

Let us not think we are any better. It is often so in this world. Gracious words often arouse only the guilty consciences of men and cause them to want to harm the one who reminds them of their sin. Christ was demanding of those people—as He demands of us—not only acknowledgment of His claims but acceptance of His Person. The first three verses of chapter 61 tell of the mission of the Messiah, and what a wonderful mission it was! Here was One who brought "good news"; One who proclaimed a far greater deliverance than any deliverance from Babylon or other earthly enemies; One who opened the prison house of sin and invited the poor prisoners to come out into the glorious liberty of the children of God; One who announced "the favorable year of the LORD," a long, gracious "year" that is even now continuing. But that same One will also bring "the day of vengeance of our God." There is no doubt significance in the relative use of the terms *year* and *day*. The word *year* is used for the time of grace, because it is God's good pleasure to extend it (cf. 2 Pet. 3:9) so that many more may come to the Savior. The word *day* is used for the time of judgment, as indeed it is often used in the prophets, particularly in the expression "the day of the LORD."

Verses 4-8 describe the benefits of the Messiah's mission to Israel. Both advents of Christ are in the narrative. When He came the first time He presented Himself to Israel as King by riding on a donkey (a symbol of peaceful rule). The "favorable year of the LORD" has continued potentially for all—both Jews and Gentiles —who will accept and trust Him. But when He comes again, as He is pictured in Revelation 19, He will be riding on a white horse (a symbol of warfare). That this is correct is confirmed by the passage itself: "In righteousness He judges and wages war" (Rev. 19:11). When He comes in that "day of vengeance" (described in Isaiah 63, 2 Thessalonians 1, and in a number of passages in Revelation) He will also "comfort all who mourn" (v. 2), no doubt primarily an allusion to the godly remnant in Israel who will see Him in His glorious second coming and accept Him with genuine mourning for their sins (Rev. 1:7). "Blessed are those who mourn," Jesus said, "for they shall be comforted" (Matt. 5:4). That the allusion in the present Isaiah passage is particularly to Israel is indicated in verse 3 by the phrase "in Zion." Remember that Zion is *Zion*, not the church, certain creeds and catechisms, and many hymn writers to the contrary notwithstanding.

There may be a partial reference in verse 4 and following to the return from Babylon, but the present writers agree with Ryrie and others that the description is of "conditions in the millennial kingdom." One who takes these prophecies literally and visits the land of Israel today cannot but rejoice at the changes that are to come in that land. It holds great interest even now for the Christian because so many Bible heroes and heroines lived their lives for God there, and especially because it was the land of the Lord Jesus in the "days of His flesh." In that future day, after the Lord Jesus has put down all opposition and reigns in personal presence and power, the land—although the same locale—will be almost unrecognizable because of the glories that will be bestowed on it, as Isaiah 62 testifies.

At Mount Sinai long ago God proposed to the people of Israel through Moses that if they would obey Him He would make them a "kingdom of priests" (Ex. 19:5-6). Israel failed, and what God at that time promised to Israel conditionally He later proclaimed unconditionally to the church (1 Pet. 2:9). That does not mean that Israel has been completely and finally rejected. The Bible is full of promises of the restoration of Israel. After its long failure Israel "will be called the priests of the LORD" (v. 6). The following promises show how Israel is to be enriched in that coming millennial time. The mention of the "double portion" (v. 7) forms a contrast to the "double" that Israel will have received for all her sins (Isa. 40:2).

Verse 9 indicates the effect of the Messiah's mission on the whole world, following its effect on Israel in the preceding verses.

There is genuine uncertainty among commentators about the identity of the speaker in verse 10. Some contend that it is the same one as in verse 1, the Messiah Himself. Others maintain that Christ is never spoken of as putting on "garments of salvation" or a "robe of righteousness," because He is the Savior who does not need salvation and is intrinsically and absolutely righteous; certainly not in need of being clothed with righteousness. If it is He who is speaking, He is evidently identifying Himself with the godly remnant and speaking as their representative. Some believe the Messiah is pictured as clothing Himself with the garments of the high priest (cf. Ex. 39:28 and Ezek. 44:18). These two closing verses of the chapter sing forth the joy of the Lord (cf. Phil. 4:4 and Hab. 3:17-19). The analogy of a wedding is used a number of times in Scripture. Righteousness and praise are truly from the Lord through His Servant, the Messiah.

Jerusalem a Praise in the Earth (62:1-12)

This chapter describes the restoration of Israel in beautiful, figurative language. Who is the speaker here? Many commentators say it is Isaiah. Delitzsch takes it to be the Lord. Perhaps it is the Messiah as at the beginning of chapter 61. He is constrained to speak; it is as though He says, "I can *not* keep silent."

The Jerusalem described here will have come a long way from the "Sodom" of chapter 1. It is Jerusalem as God wants it to be and as He will cause it to be. The "new name" (v. 2) will be in keeping with the exalted character of Israel that will then be revealed. It will be the Lord's determination and designation. Delitzsch points out that the verb means "to designate in a signal and distinguishing manner."[5] Jerusalem will be a "crown of beauty in the hand of the Lord" (v. 3). God's original intention for Israel was that it should be both a priestly and a kingly nation. That intention will be fulfilled in the millennium (cf. Ex. 19:6). The new

5. Delitzsch, 2:435.

names that God will give to the city and the land will emphasize the contrast to their former forsaken and desolate condition.

A contrast is drawn between "forsaken" (*azubah*) and "desolate" (*shemamah*) on the one hand and "My delight is in her" (*hepsi-bah*) and "married" (*beulah*) on the other. Azubah and Hephzibah were in use as actual names in ancient Israel, the former being the name of King Jehoshaphat's mother (1 Kings 22:42) and the latter the name of King Manasseh's mother (2 Kings 21:1). The expression *your sons will marry you* (v. 5) is a rather strange figure of speech, yet it graphically conveys the thought that the land will be inhabited. As in Isaiah 51:17-21, Zion is seen as an abstraction separate from those who inhabit her.

The watchmen (v. 6) are the prophets and godly people in Israel. Delitzsch sees an allusion to the time after the Babylonian captivity and mentions the postexilic prophets Haggai, Zechariah, and Malachi, but the prophecy certainly goes far beyond that time. The idea of reminding the Lord alludes to the persistence of the "watchmen." They are reminding God of something He "appears" to have forgotten (cf. 43:26). God delights in having His people call on Him in that way. The true character of intercession is vividly brought out in verse 7 (cf. the parable of the importunate widow in Luke 18). People are told in the Scripture to pray for Jerusalem (see, for example, Ps. 122:6). It may seem incredible to some, but God's purpose is to make Jerusalem "a praise in the earth." The Lord's "right hand" and "strong arm" are symbolic of His power and strength. His very character is at stake, for He has promised by an oath that He will restore Jerusalem.

God's Word must be fulfilled, and no amount of spiritualizing or allegorizing can destroy the plain intent of it. Jerusalem cannot mean here the heavenly Jerusalem, much less the church. This Jerusalem is to be made a "praise *in the earth*." Here, as so often in Isaiah, the wheel has completely turned—judgment is past and comfort has come. God pledges His ominpotence to bring His promise to pass (cf. Deut. 28:33, 51). Israel's crops will no longer be given to their enemies. Verse 9 speaks of prosperity with thanksgiving to God and of enjoyment in prosperity.

In verse 10 the prophet, speaking to Israel, tells the people to come out of Babylonian exile (cf. 48:20; 52:11), but as usual, the passage looks beyond the return from Babylon to the final regathering of Israel out of all nations. The expression "to the end of the earth" (v. 11) is conclusive. The figure of the "highway" is used (v. 10) to picture graphically the return of the people to Zion. The "they" in verse 12 refers to men in general, who in that future day will recognize God's purpose for Israel.

THE DAY OF VENGEANCE (63:1-19)

Chapter 63 opens with a dialogue, or in modern terminology it might be called an interview. To the astonished question of the prophet, "Who is this?" the Messiah Himself answers, "I who speak in righteousness, mighty to save." The first three verses have an antiphonal character, bringing out vividly and dramatically by questions and answers the person and work of the One to whom attention is directed.

The first six verses speak of judgment by the Messiah on Edom, which is chosen as representative of Israel's enemies in general (cf. 34:6). Delitzsch comments:

> Babylon and Edom are always to be taken literally, so far as the primary meaning of the prophecy is concerned; but they are also representative, Babylon standing for the violent and tyrannical world-power, and Edom for the world as cherishing hostility and manifesting hostility to Israel as Israel, i.e., as the people of God.[6]

In the opening question the prophet seems to be asking a third person about the approaching One from Edom and Bozrah. But the coming One answers for Himself. Some have identified paronomasia here because Edom means "red" and Bozrah is related to the word for "grape gatherer." The coming One links righteousness and salvation. This is Christ in His second coming. After His reply the prophet addresses Him directly (v. 2). The further reply (v. 3) is often misunderstood and misinterpreted. The figure has often been misapplied to the death of Christ on Calvary, as though He were covered with His own blood. It is true that He suffered and died alone, but that is foreign to this context. The blood in this instance is clearly the blood of His enemies. It is a picture of judgment by Christ returning in power as He tramples

6. Ibid., p. 444.

His enemies in His wrath. This is a graphic representation of the "day of vengeance" (v. 4), previously mentioned in 61:2, but purposely omitted by the Lord Jesus in His reading in the synagogue at Nazareth.

By the time of this fulfillment the "acceptable year" (KJV) will be over; the Savior will have become the Judge. Some of the imagery of the book of Revelation is drawn from this chapter (see Rev. 14:19; 19:13; cf. Hag. 2:16 and Joel 3:13). The mention of the winepress in Revelation 14 and the portrayal of the coming of Christ in glory in Revelation 19 are echoes of this passage. The latter portion says: "And He is clothed with a robe dipped in blood; and His name is called The Word of God" (Rev. 19:13).

The "year of redemption" (v. 4), which is so closely linked with the "day of vengeance," is the long-awaited redemption of Israel that will result also in the establishment of the millennial kingdom and the lifting of the Adamic curse from the earth (cf. Rom. 8:21). Delitzsch and others refer this action to Jehovah, but it seems more accurate to apply it to the Second Person specifically, as the New Testament indicates (cf. John 5:22). Obviously, the ineffable Name—Yahweh—belongs to each and all of the Persons of the Godhead.

This is a direct intervention of God in the affairs of men and of the earth (v. 5). It is ordinarily said that God works now through His providence, which is an indirect working. In that future time He will work directly and immediately through His judgment. Therefore, that coming time is called in scores of Old Testament passages "the Day of the Lord."

Seeing that in the context of the whole of Scripture one can appreciate the prophetic import of such passages as Psalm 2: "Thou shalt break them with a rod of iron, Thou shalt shatter them like earthenware" (Ps. 2:9).

A new section begins with verse 7, praise from the godly remnant for the many blessings that God has bestowed on Israel. It is not incongruous to find the foregoing stern picture of judgment followed immediately by the mention of "the loving-kindness of the Lord." Some indeed would see only one side of the truth; misconstruing the love of God, they would deny or overlook His holiness. But right cannot triumph unless wrong is put down. And we live at present in a world of wrong. It would be most incongruous if the Savior were *not* ultimately the Judge.

Furthermore, in His judgment He is not harsh, arbitrary, or cruel, but is still the longsuffering, merciful, and gracious God. But grace that is spurned can lead only to judgment.

The judgment of evildoers will result in deliverance for the oppressed people of God. Hence this song of God's loving-kindness. There is in these verses a review of some of Israel's history, evidently in particular of the deliverance from Egypt with all its accompanying miracles and displays of God's power and glory. God is seen as sympathizing with His people in all their afflictions, feeling the afflictions as though they were His own. The "angel of His presence" (v. 9) seems to be the Angel of Yahweh, generally understood to be a theophany. "He lifted them and carried them" fits the Sinai experiences of Israel; likewise, the rebellion mentioned here is descriptive of the response of the unbelieving and complaining multitude of that time (cf. Ps. 78:40). That it is not restricted to that one time period seems clear from verse 11.

Often in the Old Testament the deliverance at the Red Sea is set forth as a measure and standard of God's power (cf. Ps. 77:20; Mic. 6:4). Here a comparison is drawn between what God did in delivering Israel from Egypt in Moses' time and what He will do in delivering them from all nations in the end time. The crossing of the Red Sea ("as on dry land," Heb. 11:29, KJV) is again referred to in verse 13. The entrance into the Promised Land is described in a beautiful figure. Delitzsch calls attention to how the people and their flocks and herds "rested and [were] refreshed after the long and wearisome march through the sandy desert, like a flock that had descended from the bare mountains to the brooks and meadows of the valley."[7]

The praise of the remnant leads to the prayer that begins in verse 15. The ground of the prayer is that God is the Father of the nation (v. 16; cf. Ex. 4:22; Deut. 32:6). Obviously, Abraham and Jacob would not disown the nation. Even if they were present and disowned the nation, God would not give up His people.

In the prayer, the people transfer to God the responsibility for their plight, but He has only withdrawn His rejected grace. That is analogous to what God told Isaiah (Isa. 6) when He indicated the prophet would have a hardening ministry. Israel's time of enjoy-

7. Ibid., p. 459.

ment of the land was comparatively short when compared to the long dispersion. So severe has been the judgment that the relationship between God and Israel seems not only to be broken off, but never to have existed. The climax of the prayer, which comes at the beginning of the next chapter, is the expression of a strong desire for God to manifest Himself.

THE PRAYER OF THE REMNANT (64:1-12)

The first verse of chapter 64 in English versions is the last part of 63:19 in the Hebrew text. Yet it fits most suitably with what follows.

The closing chapters of Isaiah (64-66) contain a mingling of condemnation and glory in a manner the careful reader of the prophecy has become accustomed to. The great panorama of the second part of the book sweeps before us in its portrayal of deliverance from Babylon as a foretaste of an even greater deliverance; in its description of the Messiah, the Servant of the Lord, through whom deliverance comes; and in its building up to this climax of the glorious future for the nation of Israel. All the blessing is through the Servant, who is also the avenger, the executor of the wrath of God. Chapter 64 continues the aspirations of the godly remnant of Israel; chapter 65 contains the answer of the Lord to their prayer; and the concluding chapter describes God's final judgments in the restoration of Israel and vengeance on the transgressors. There is no suspense in this story for one who follows it from the beginning, for the end is fully known. But each time the story is retold and the dominant themes are repeated, there is a new impact on the soul.

The members of the godly remnant of the nation, acutely aware of God's almighty power in the past history of the nation, express their earnest longing for a repetition in their own time: "Oh, that Thou wouldst rend the heavens and come down" (64:1).

That may be thought of as a universal longing of God's people through the ages. Even though believers know that they walk by faith, not by sight (2 Cor. 5:7), there is somehow always the desire for sight, for observing God's intervention in human history. We are aware of His providential dealings, but we want also His immediate judgmental dealings. Other Scriptures carry the refrain "How long, O Lord?" (cf. e.g., Rev. 6:10). Now the nations mock at the thought of God; then they will "tremble at [His] presence"

(v. 2). Ryrie speaks of that as "the kind of prayer Israel will pray during the Tribulation days."[8]

Those who pray know that God is able and that the things of God are far beyond human experience and understanding. Paul, under the guidance of the Holy Spirit, makes use of the thought of verse 4 in what he writes to the Corinthians: "But just as it is written, 'Things which eye has not seen and ear has not heard, and which have not entered the heart of man, all that God has prepared for those who love Him'" (1 Cor. 2:9).

Does that mean we can never know those things? Not at all: "For to us God revealed them through the Spirit; for the Spirit searches all things, even the depths of God" (1 Cor. 2:10).

As always, the godly identify themselves with the nation at large and confess their sin to God (v. 5). They acknowledge that God's judgments have come because of sin, as Daniel did in Babylon near the close of the captivity (Dan. 9:3-11).

The righteous deeds are likened to soiled garments that are thrown away as useless (v. 6). The last part of verse 6, which speaks of the wind taking them away, is reminiscent of the description of the ungodly in Psalm 1: "But they are like chaff which the wind drives away" (Ps. 1:4).

Somehow those who know God best are most conscious of their own sinfulness. Isaiah himself found that to be true (Isa. 6). Those in this passage who confess their sin know they cannot base their appeal to God on any merit of their own—that indeed they have no merit at all. Even their righteous deeds are worthless in God's sight. On what then can they base their appeal? On the only ground that anyone can ever find in any dispensation under any circumstances—the mercy and grace of God.

God is addressed as the Father of the nation and as the Potter who has fashioned the clay (cf. Jer. 18:6; Rom. 9:21-24). This figure emphasizes the absolute right of the Lord to do whatever He pleases with His people. The remnant in their prayer of confession know they have no *rights* before God, but they are not asking for rights (that would result in condemnation) but for God's mercy— His lovingkindness.

The desolation of Zion and Jerusalem must be taken literally. They are mourning the destruction of the city and especially the beautiful Temple that Solomon had built so long before.

8. Ryrie, p. 1108.

CONDEMNATION AND GLORY (65:1-25)

In His reply to the prayer of the remnant God brings out the fact of Israel's rebelliousness. The Gentiles, who were far off where privileges were concerned, were actually seeking God (v. 1), while His special people Israel were rebelling against Him.

The description of the people of Israel here (v. 2) is similar to that in the very first chapter of the prophecy (1:2). God reiterates His purpose to recompense their rebelliousness. Their self-righteousness, self-deceit and hypocrisy ("holier than you," v. 5) are characteristic of their sinful attitude. While professing holiness they lived godless lives, disobeying even the most elemental of God's commandments. They also were engaging in idol worship, in the forbidden practice of seeking communication with the dead (as in modern spiritism), and in breaking the dietary laws that God had given to Israel. That is only a representative list of their transgressions.

The Holy Spirit's application of the opening verses of this chapter, as it is seen in the New Testament, is instructive:

And Isaiah is very bold and says, "I was found by those who sought Me not, I became manifest to those who did not ask for Me." But as for Israel He says, "All the day long I have stretched out My hands to a disobedient and obstinate people." [Rom. 10:20-21]

God's stretching forth His hands (obviously an anthropomorphism) is a clear indication of His personal yearning for the love and obedience of those people whom He has chosen.

Yet as the New Testament application goes on to show, that does not mean God has cast away His people (Rom. 11:1-6). There is always the remnant, the true Israel, the godly "tenth" that "shall return" (Isa. 6:13, KJV). That remnant is in view in verses 8-10. God will not "destroy them all," but will "bring forth a seed" to inherit the promises. The succeeding verses paint the contrast of condemnation and glory. Addressing the rebellious and ungodly, God shows how their judgment is in contrast to the blessings on His servants (vv. 13-16). A series of five striking contrasts, the first four introduced by the emphatic exclamation "Behold!" stresses the coming glories and the coming condemnation.

The chapter closes with further description of kingdom blessings. Some difference of opinion exists about the mention of "new heavens and a new earth" (v. 17). Is that a reference to the millennial kingdom or a look ahead into the eternal state? Undoubtedly, the greater part of the description in the paragraph pertains to the millennium, for death will still be a reality in the time described, even though the life span will be greatly increased (v. 20). No doubt Ryrie's thought is appropriate: "A description of the millennial kingdom, which is preliminary to the *new heavens and a new earth* (v. 17)."[9]

It is difficult to understand the amillennial commentators who do not believe in a literal, earthly kingdom of the Messiah but nevertheless talk about a messianic age. Obviously, they can not carry the existence of death into heaven. But what do they mean by the messianic age? If this present age is the messianic age, as some avow, we are not seeing the results pictured here. Young, whose commentary is a work of brilliant scholarship, is understandably sparse here.

One can only conclude that according to that interpretation this can only be an idealized, nonliteral set of events. What we need to see is that a full-orbed interpretation of Scripture must be based on literalism, and that God's total plan of redemption includes not only the salvation of a great multitude of individuals but also the redemption of this ruined earth (Rom. 8:21). The successful dominion over the earth by the Lord Jesus Christ must replace the dominion lost by Adam's fall. On this same planet where the first Adam failed, the last Adam must assuredly succeed. "For He must reign until He has put all His enemies under His feet. The last enemy that will be abolished is death" (1 Cor. 15:25-26).

The Scriptures are clear that in the millennium there will be the resurrected, glorified saints both of the Old Testament time and of the church age who will be associated with the Lord Jesus in His reign over the earth, as well as the unglorified subjects of the kingdom. The latter will be the "sheep" on the Lord's "right hand" described in Matthew 25:33-34 as living on earth at the Lord's return in glory to whom He says: "Come, you who are blessed of My Father, inherit the kingdom prepared for you from the foundation of the world" (Matt. 25:34).

For the unglorified the natural processes of life and of death will

9. Ibid., p. 1110.

go on, for this is an earthly, not a heavenly setting, although conditions will be much more favorable for living than ever before because the Lord Jesus will be personally reigning over the earth and Satan will be bound. Israel will be the leading nation of the earth and will partake of the blessings enumerated in Isaiah and in other parts of Scripture.

The closing verse of the chapter (v. 25) carries one back in thought to the similar description of the millennium in Isaiah 11. To view this as merely an idealized portrait of spiritual conditions is to do injustice to the straightforward statement of Scripture. It will be a glorious day when these words are fulfilled: "They shall do no evil or harm in all My holy mountain." As in chapter 2 and elsewhere the "mountain" refers to God's kingdom, and the various references to it show that it will be a universal kingdom. Carrying out that same thought, Daniel speaks of the stone that "became a great mountain and filled the whole earth" (Dan. 2:35).

PEACE LIKE A RIVER (66:1-24)

The closing chapter (66) describes the "peace . . . like a river" (v. 12) that will characterize the Lord's kingdom. Its opening verses were quoted by Stephen in his address before the Jewish Council (Acts 7:49-50) to bring out the truth of God's omnipresence. God cannot be contained in any building, no matter how magnificent (Acts 17:24). Solomon realized that when he dedicated the Temple to God (1 Kings 8:27; 2 Chron. 2:6; 6:18).

The ungodly are warned that because of their continuance in sin their very sacrifices to God at the Temple are sinful (v. 3; cf. 1:12-15). As Ryrie says, "Ritualistic offerings apart from a change of heart (v. 2) are as abominable to God as murder or offering unclean animals."[10]

Those who have the interests of Jerusalem at heart are called upon by God to rejoice with her in her glory. The Lord promises that He will "extend peace to her like a river" (v. 12).

Along with that peace, however, is the Lord's indignation toward the unrepentant and unbelieving. He will "execute judgment by fire" (v. 16). God's glory will be declared among the nations. The closing verses of the book give the solemn warning of the destiny of God's enemies. The Lord Jesus alluded to the last

10. Ibid., p. 1111.

verse of Isaiah in describing the eternal punishment of the lost (Mark 9:48).

God's glory is certainly seen in the book of Isaiah. From beginning to the end He is exalted. The believer can rejoice in the salvation of the Lord, which will ultimately be extended to the ends of the earth.

Appendix 1

An Inductive Validation of the Central Theme of Isaiah

In Isaiah, as in the Old Testament as a whole, it is difficult to find a central theme from which all the material flows. At first, it appears that there should be two central themes: one for chapters 1-39 and another for chapters 40-66. Chapters 1-39 seem to speak primarily of judgment while chapters 40-66 speak of comfort. That may help to account for the views of some modern critics who want to split the book in two to accommodate two different authors.

Redemption or pardoning from sins does not seem to be broad enough to fit the description of Isaiah, which tells of a change in the order of nature (11:6-9; 55:12-13). A broader term such as "restoration" needs to be employed to describe the changes in the whole order of the cosmos. Throughout the book reference is made to Yahweh's standard which has been broken time and time again not only by Israel, but also by the other nations of the world. The sections dealing with the blessing of the kingdom show a restoration of Yahweh's created order. He did not create the world "a waste" (45:18). The Servant's role will be to deliver justice or order to the world. The Lord promises Israel that it will be restored and smelted and then Jerusalem will be called a city of righteousness (1:24-26).

The central theme therefore is seen as "Yahweh's restoration of His created order," often expressed in the commentary in Isaiah's language: Salvation of Yahweh through His Servant to the ends of the earth. It is amazing how much restoration and salvation can be seen in chapters 1-39, which upon first reading seem so full of judgment.

BOOK ONE—CHAPTERS 1-39
YAHWEH'S INDICTMENT OF THE NATION (1:1—6:13)

Chapter 1 is a lawsuit against the nation which shows the justification for Yahweh's action of judgment. But even in the lawsuit there is a major section of restoration of the nation (1:24-31).

Chapters 2-4 are a contrast between the future restored nation (2:1-4) and the present sinful nation (2:5—4:1). But chapter 4 closes with a promise of holy survivors who are restored (4:2-6).

Chapter 5 is an indictment of the present sinful condition of the nation, while chapter 6 is Isaiah's response not only to Yahweh's indictment but to Yahweh Himself. The section ends with a note of hope—a holy seed (6:13).

PROPHECIES OF DELIVERANCE (7:1—12:6)

This entire section deals with the coming deliverance of the nation both in this historical context and in the distant future. Not only will the nation have deliverance from the Syrian-Israel alliance (7:3-9; 8:1-l5; 9:7—10:4), but there also will be the rise of a new glorious empire that will take the place of the Assyrian Empire, which will fall (11:1—12:6). The future deliverance of the nation will come through One who will come from Galilee, whose kingdom is eternal (9:1-7). The remnant will be regathered a second time (11:11-12) and they will sing a song of thanksgiving because they will be with the source of their salvation (12:1-6, esp. v. 3).

JUDGMENT ON THE NATIONS (13:1—23:18)

Even in the section of judgment on the nations there is a theme of restoration. Israel will again be in the land, ruling over peoples who have oppressed it (14:1-2). Moab will come to Israel for protection, justice, and the establishment of order (16:1-5). Gifts will be brought to Mt. Zion (18:7). Judah will control Egypt (19:16-17) and part of Egypt will swear allegiance to the God of Israel (19:18). The worship of the true God in Egypt will signal peace on earth (19:19-25).

PUNISHMENT AND KINGDOM BLESSING (24:1—27:13)

Chapters 25-27 are full of the salvation of the Lord and the restoration of both the people and the world order. God preserves His people (25:1-12) and is praised by the redeemed (26:1-27).

The evil system is judged (27:1) and the remnant is restored (27:2-13). It is important to notice that judgment comes on the nation for a refining purpose (27:7-13).

THE WOES (28:1—33:24)

At the end of the three sections of woe there is a word of comfort: judgment will only last for a short while and is designed to purge the people (28:23-29); future things will be different and a remnant will glorify the Lord (29:17-24); and the Lord will bless His people and protect them (30:23-26; 31:4-9). The final section (32:1—33:24) describes the reign of the just King in a time of justice and righteousness.

VENGEANCE AND BLESSING (34:1—35:10)

Even in the vengeance section there is a note that a remnant will be gathered together (34:16-17). The land will then be free from the curse and the remnant will dwell with everlasting joy on their heads (35:1-10).

HISTORICAL INTERLUDE (36:1—39:8)

The Lord promises immediate deliverance in the present historical situation (37:30-32). The primary purpose of this section seems to be to function as a hinge to lead the reader to the Babylonian section, Book Two.

BOOK TWO—CHAPTERS 40-66
THE DELIVERANCE OF GOD'S PEOPLE (40:1—48:22)

The entire section deals with deliverance and salvation. In the immediate historical context God will deliver the people from their captivity in Babylon. In the more distant future He will change the entire world (41:17-20). His Servant is on a mission of salvation to the Gentiles (42:1-7). In His mission He will effect justice on the earth—restore order to the earth (42:1-4). The Lord promises to regather His unworthy servant Israel to the land (43:14—44:5). He uses a Gentile power to restore Temple worship in the land (44:24-28). He promises that the Gentile world will bow down to a redeemed Israel, for they are His chosen people (45:14-19).

RESTORATION BY THE SUFFERING SERVANT (49:1—57:21)

This section overwhelmingly deals with salvation and restoration. The Servant will take salvation to the Gentiles and then at the proper time Israel will return (49:1-13). The Lord assures the deserted land that it will be restored (49:14-26). The righteous remnant will be exalted (51:1—52:12). The Servant is exalted and receives His deserved place because He voluntarily did the will of God (52:13—53:12). The Servant's salvation includes both Israel (54:1-17) and the Gentiles (55:1-13).

THE REALIZATION OF RESTORATION (58:1—66:24)

The Lord requires obedience (58:1-14), and since the nation is depraved, salvation and restoration must come by God's initiative (59:1-21). In the period of salvation there will be prosperity and peace on the earth for those whom the Lord has redeemed (60:1-22). The Anointed One will come (61:1-11) and will clothe the redeemed with a robe of righteousness (vv. 10-11). The Lord describes a new kingdom which will be set up (65:17-25). The Lord promises to fulfill His promises that are in the Abrahamic covenant and restore Israel to a prominent place (66:7-21).

Appendix 2

Quotations from Isaiah in the New Testament

The list given here contains identifiable quotations of Isaiah in the New Testament. It does not contain every allusion that the New Testament writers make to the text of Isaiah.

I. IN THE ORDER OF THE NEW TESTAMENT BOOKS

New Testament Reference	Explanatory Introduction	Isaiah Reference
1. Matthew 1:23	"the prophet"	7:14
2. 3:3	"the prophet Isaiah"	40:3
3. 4:15-16	"Isaiah the prophet"	9:1-2
4. 8:17	"Isaiah the prophet"	53:4
5. 12:18-21	"Isaiah the prophet"	42:1-4
6. 13:14-15	"the prophecy of Isaiah"	6:9-10
7. 15:8-9	"Isaiah"	29:13
8. 21:13	"it is written"	56:7
9. Mark 1:3	"in the Prophets"	40:3
10. 4:12	"in order that"	6:9-10
11. 7:6-7	"Isaiah"	29:13
12. 9:44, 46, 48	"into the unquenchable fire"	66:24
13. 11:17	"Is it not written?"	56:7
14. 15:28	"the Scripture"	53:12
15. Luke 3:4-6	"Isaiah the prophet"	40:3-5
16. 4:18-19	"the prophet Isaiah"	61:1-2
17. 8:10	"in order that"	6:9
18. 19:46	"it is written"	56:7
19. 22:37	"this which is written"	53:12

177

20. John 1:23	"the prophet Isaiah"	40:3
21. 6:45	"it is written in the prophets"	54:13
22. 12:38	"Isaiah the prophet"	53:1
23. 12:40	"Isaiah"	6:10
24. Acts 7:49-50	"the prophet"	66:1-2
25. 8:32-33	"Isaiah the prophet"	53:7-8
26. 13:34	"He has spoken thus"	55:3
27. 13:47	"for thus the Lord has commanded us"	49:6
28. 8:26-27	"Isaiah the prophet"	6:9-10
29. Romans 2:24	"just as it is written"	52:5
30. 3:15-17	"it is written"	59:7-8
31. 9:27-28	"Isaiah"	10:22-23
32. 9:29	"Isaiah"	1:9
33. 9:33	"it is written"	8:14; 28:16
34. 10:11	"the Scripture says"	28:16
35. 10:15	"it is written"	52:7
36. 10:16	"Isaiah"	53:1
37. 10:20	"Isaiah"	65:1
38. 10:21	"he" (Isaiah)	65:2
39. 11:8	"it is written"	29:10
40. 11:26-27	"it is written"	59:20-21
41. 11:34	"for"	40:13
42. 14:11	"it is written"	45:23
43. 15:12	"Isaiah"	11:10
44. 15:21	"it is written"	52:15
45. 1 Cor. 1:19	"it is written"	29:14
46. 2:9	"it is written"	64:4
47. 2:16	"for"	40:13
48. 14:21	"in the law it is written"	28:11-12
49. 15:32	"if the dead are not raised"	22:13
50. 15:54	"the saying that is written"	25:8
51. 2 Cor. 6:2	"for He says"	49:8
52. 6:17	"therefore"	52:11
53. Galatians 4:27	"it is written"	54:1
54. Hebrews 2:13	"and again"	8:17
55. 2:13	"and again"	8:18
56. 1 Pet. 1:24-25	"for"	40:6-8
57. 2:6	"contained in Scripture"	28:16
58. 2:8	"and"	8:14

59. 2:22	53:9
60. 3:14	8:12
61. Revelation 3:7	22:22

II. IN THE ORDER IN WHICH THEY APPEAR IN ISAIAH

Isaiah	New Testament Reference
1:9	Romans 9:29
6:9	Luke 8:10
6:9-10	Matthew 13:14-15
	Mark 4:12
	Acts 28:26-27
6:10	John 12:40
7:14	Matthew 1:23
8:12	1 Peter 3:14
8:14	Romans 9:33
	1 Peter 2:8
8:17	Hebrews 2:13
8:18	Hebrews 2:13
9:1-2	Matthew 4:15-16
10:22-23	Romans 9:27-28
11:10	Romans 15:12
22:13	1 Corinthians 15:32
22:22	Revelation 3:7
25:8	1 Corinthians 15:54
28:11-12	1 Corinthians 14:21
28:16	Romans 9:33
	Romans 10:11
	1 Peter 2:6
29:10	Romans 11:8
29:13	Matthew 15:8-9
	Mark 7:6-7
29:14	1 Corinthians 1:19
40:3	Matthew 3:3
	Mark 1:3
	John 1:23
40:3-5	Luke 3:4-6
40:6-8	1 Peter 1:24,25
40:13	Romans 11:34
	1 Corinthians 2:16
42:1-4	Matthew 12:18-21

45:23	Romans 14:11
49:6	Acts 13:47
49:8	2 Corinthians 6:2
52:5	Romans 2:24
52:7	Romans 10:15
52:11	2 Corinthians 6:17
52:15	Romans 15:21
53:1	John 12:38
	Romans 10:16
53:4	Matthew 8:17
53:7-8	Acts 8:32-33
53:9	1 Peter 2:22
53:12	Mark 15:28
	Luke 22:37
54:1	Galatians 4:27
54:13	John 6:45
55:3	Acts 13:34
56:7	Matthew 21:13
	Mark 11:17
	Luke 19:46
59:7-8	Romans 3:15-17
59:20-21	Romans 11:26-27
61:1-2	Luke 4:18-19
64:4	1 Corinthians 2:9
65:1	Romans 10:20
65:2	Romans 10:21
66:1-2	Acts 7:49-50
66:24	Mark 9:44, 46, 48

Selective Bibliography

Alexander, Joseph Addison. *Commentary on the Prophecies of Isaiah.* Reprint. Grand Rapids: Zondervan, 1971.

Allis, Oswald T. *The Unity of Isaiah: A Study in Prophecy.* Philadelphia: Presbyterian and Reformed, 1972.

Anstey, Martin. *The Romance of Bible Chronology.* 2 vols. London: Marshall, 1913.

Archer, Gleason L. *A Survey of Old Testament Introduction.* Rev. ed. Chicago: Moody, 1974.

Barnes, Albert. *Notes on the Old Testament, Explanatory and Practical: Isaiah.* 2 vols. Grand Rapids: Baker, 1950.

Baron, David. *The Servant of Jehovah: An Exposition of Isaiah 53.* London: Morgan and Scott, 1922.

Bultema, Harry. *Commentary on Isaiah.* Translated from the Dutch by Cornelius Lambregtse. Grand Rapids: Kregel, 1981.

Calvin, John. *Commentary on the Book of the Prophet Isaiah.* 4 vols. Translated by William Pringle. Grand Rapids: Eerdmans, 1947.

————.*The Gospel According to Isaiah: Seven Sermons on Isaiah 53.* Translated by Leroy Nixon. Grand Rapids: Eerdmans, 1953.

Delitzsch, Franz. *Biblical Commentary on the Prophecies of Isaiah.* 2 vols. Translated by James Martin. Clark's Foreign Theological Library, Fourth Series. Edinburgh: T. and T. Clark, 1881.

Gray, George B. *A Critical and Exegetical Commentary on the Book of Isaiah.* The International Critical Commentary. Edinburgh: T. & T. Clark, 1912.

Ironside, H. A. *Expository Notes on the Prophet Isaiah*. Neptune, N.J.: Loizeaux, 1952.

Jamieson, Robert; Fausset, A. R.; and Brown, David. *A Commentary Critical, Experimental and Practical on the Old and New Testaments*. 6 vols. Vol. 3, *Job-Isaiah*, by A. R. Fausset. Grand Rapids: Eerdmans, 1945.

Jennings, F. C. *Studies in Isaiah*. Neptune, N.J.: Loizeaux, n.d.

Josephus, Flavius. *Complete Works*. Translated by William Whiston. Philadelphia: John E. Potter, n.d.

Kelly, William. *An Exposition of the Book of Isaiah*. Reprint. Oak Park, Ill.: Bible Truth, 1975.

Lange, John Peter, ed. *Commentary on the Holy Scriptures: Critical, Doctrinal and Homiletical*. 25 vols. Vol 11, *Isaiah*, by C. W. Edward Naegelsbach. Grand Rapids: Zondervan, n.d.

Leupold, H. C. *Exposition of Isaiah*. Grand Rapids: Baker, 1971.

MacRae, Allan A. *The Gospel of Isaiah*. Chicago: Moody, 1977.

Martin, Alfred. *Isaiah, "The Salvation of Jehovah": A Survey of the Book of Isaiah the Prophet*. Chicago: Moody, 1956.

Orelli, C. von. *The Prophecies of Isaiah*. Translated by J. S. Banks. Edinburgh: T. and T. Clark, 1889.

Redpath, Alan. *The Plan of Deliverance: Studies in the Prophecies of Isaiah*. 2 vols. Old Tappan, N.J.: Revell, 1972-74.

Robinson, George L. "Isaiah," in *The International Standard Bible Encyclopedia*. 5 vols. Grand Rapids: Eerdmans, 1939. 3:1495-1508.

———. *The Book of Isaiah in Fifteen Studies*. Grand Rapids: Baker, 1954.

Thiele, Edwin R. *A Chronology of the Hebrew Kings*. Grand Rapids: Zondervan, 1977.

———. *The Mysterious Numbers of the Hebrew Kings: A Reconstruction of the Chronology of the Kingdoms of Israel and Judah*. Chicago: U. of Chicago, 1955.

Vine, W. E. *Isaiah: Prophecies, Promises, Warnings*. Grand Rapids: Zondervan, 1971.

Young, Edward J. *The Book of Isaiah*. 3 vols. *The New International Commentary on the Old Testament*. Grand Rapids: Eerdmans, 1969-72.

Scripture Index

OLD TESTAMENT

Genesis
3:15   72, 133, 139
11   122
11:1-9   69
15:5   128
19:1-29   37
19:37   74
24:43   55

Exodus
2:8   55
3:12   54
3:14   20
4:8   54
4:22   165
12:11   130
12:36   130
14:19-20   130
19:5-6   160
19:6   161
21:10   43
33:20   47
39:28   161
40:34-35   48

Leviticus
26   37

Numbers
2:16   46
22:20   49
35:30   58

Deuteronomy
6:12   17
6:16   54
14:2   112
17:6   58
17:16   88
19:15   58
23:1   147
23:3   74
25:1   127
28   37
28:13   40
28:33   162
28:51   162
32   36
32:6   165
32:15   117
33:5   117
33:26   117

Joshua
10:13-14   103

Judges
6:34   157
13:18   60

Ruth
4:10   74
4:13   74
4:22   74

1 Samuel
17:56   55
20:22   55

2 Samuel
7   35
7:1-29   62
7:4-17   120

1 Kings
1:27   155
8:10-11   48
8:27   46, 170
13:2   118
16:24   85

19:18	49	1:7-11	130	115:4-8		114
22:42	162	2:1-70	50, 116	118:22		87
		4:2, 10	53	122:6		162
2 Kings		7:1-10	116	132:7		155
14:22	52					
15-20	17	Nehemiah		Proverbs		
15:1	17	2:1-10	116	3:34		42
15:3	17			20:1		86
15:19	72	Job		23:29-35		86
15:34	17	1:8	48	30:19		55
16:2	17	38	108			
16:2-4	54	38:7	73	Song of Solomon		
16:5	52	42:5-6	48	1:3		55
16:7-9	53			6:8		55
18-19	92	Psalms				
18-20	97	1:4	167	Isaiah		
18:1	98	2	40, 92, 142	1		27
18:3	17	2:5	94	1-39	19, 21, 24,	
19	17, 24, 97	2:9	64, 164		28, 30, 33	
19:9	76	14:1	101	1:1	18, 33, 34,	
19:31	62	19:1	109			107
21:1	162	22	133-34	1:1—6:13	30, 33	
22:1—23:30	35	23:1	107, 139	1:1—35:10		29
		34:6	154	1:1-31		33
1 Chronicles		42:1	66	1:2	36, 39, 89,	
28:2	155	46	40, 146		106, 168	
		46:9	42	1:2-23		33
2 Chronicles		68:26	55	1:3		36
2:6	170	69	133	1:4	36, 37	
6:18	170	72	142, 146	1:5		37
9:20	27, 155	76:10	63	1:7		37
11:16	52	77:20	165	1:9	24, 37	
26-32	17	78:40	165	1:10		37
26:16	17	80:1	107, 139	1:12-15		170
28:5-15	53	80:8	43	1:13		37
29-32	97	85:10	64	1:15		38
32:31	103	95:7	107	1:16		38
36:22-23	119	98	146	1:18		38
		99:5	155	1:20	38, 24, 152	
Ezra		100:3	107	1:21		38
1:1-11	119	115:3	121	1:24-26		20

1:24-31	33, 38
1:26	39
1:27	39
2	170
2:1—4:6	33
2:1-4	33, 39
2:4	41
2:5—3:36	41
2:7-8	24, 42
2:12	41, 42
2:17	42
2:18	42
2:21	42
3:4	42
3:8-9	42
3:14-15	42
4:1	43
4:1-6	33, 43
4:2	43, 64
4:3	43
4:5	43
4:6	43
5	27, 84
5:1	43
5:1-6	34
5:1-30	33, 34, 43
5:7	28, 43
5:7-30	34
5:8-10	43
5:11-14	43
5:15-17	44
5:18-19	44
5:20	44
5:21	44
5:22-23	44
5:24	44
5:25	44, 62
5:26-30	44
6	15, 29, 44, 45, 165, 167
6:1	17, 18, 45
6:1-4	34
6:1-13	24, 33, 34, 44
6:2	47
6:3	5, 12, 24, 46, 47
6:5	48, 49
6:5-7	34
6:7	49
6:8	49
6:8-13	34
6:9	49
6:13	49
7-12	29, 66, 87
7:1	18, 33, 511
7:1—12:6	30
7:1-9	51
7:1-17	51, 52
7:2	52, 5
7:3	19, 5
7:7	5
7:8	5
7:9	5
7:10-17	5
7:11	53, 5
7:13	5
7:14	25, 55, 61, 66, 87, 92, 107, 126, 153
7:18—8:22	52, 57
7:20	57
7:1—12:6	51
8:1-4	58
8:2	58
8:3	19, 55
8:8	58
8:9	24
8:9-10	58
8:9-15	58
8:10	58
8:11-15	58
8:13	58
8:14	87
8:18	19, 54, 58
9	115, 153
9:1-2	59
9:1-7	52, 59
9:2	60
9:6	60, 87
9:6-7	40, 55, 92
9:7	62, 64
9:8—10:34	52, 62
9:12, 21	62
9:13	63
10-12	135
10:4	62
10:12	63
10:20	63
10:20-22	24
11:1	25, 63, 92, 133
11:1-16	52, 63
11:2	64
11:4	64
11:5	64
11:6	65
11:7	65
11:9	47, 65
11:11, 16	24, 65
11:12	65
11:16	24, 65, 66, 95
12	27, 115, 146
12:1	66
12:1-2	66
12:1-6	52, 66
12:2	66
12:3	66
12:3-6	66
12:6	66
13	121
13-14	122

13-23	29, 67	19:1—20:6	68, 76	25:8	83
13:1	70	19:1-4	76, 77	26:1-19	82, 83
13:1—14:27	68, 69	19:1-25	76	26:3	83
13:1—23:18	30, 68	19:4	76	26:4	84, 87
13:1-16	69, 70	19:5-10	77	26:20	84
13:4-5	71	19:11-15	77	26:20—27:13	82,
13:4-8	72	19:13	77		84
13:6-9	71	19:16-17	77	26:21	84
13:10-16	71	19:18	77	27:2-6	84
13:17-22	69, 71	19:19-22	77	27:6	84
13:19-22	70	19:23-25	77	28-33	29
14:1-2	71	20:1	18	28:1	86
14:3-27	69, 71	20:1-6	77	28:1—33:24	30,
14:9-11	72	20:6	77		85
14:12-14	72	21:1-10	68, 77	28:1-13	85
14:12-17	73	21:9	77	28:5	24, 86
14:12-21	72	21:11-12	66, 78	28:7	86
14:14	73	21:13-17	68, 78	28:9-10	86
14:15	73	21:17	24	28:11	86
14:22, 30	24	22:1-11	78	28:14	86
14:24-27	70, 72,	22:1-25	68, 78	28:14-29	85, 86
	74	22:12-14	78, 79	28:15	87
14:25	72	22:14	78	28:16	25, 87
14:28	18	22:15-19	78	29:1	87
14:28-32	68, 74	22:15-25	78	29:1-24	85, 87
14:29	74	22:25	79	29:2	88
14:31-32	74	23:1-18	68, 79	29:13	88
15:1—16:14	68, 74	23:1-7	79	29:17-24	88
15:9	24	23:8-18	79	30:1	89
16:1	74	23:15-18	79	30:1—31:9	85, 88
16:1-9	75	24-27	29, 81	30:15	89
16:6	74	24:1—27:13	30, 82	30:31	89
16:6-12	75	24:1-23	82	31:3	89
16:14	24, 74	24:3	82	31:4	89
17:1-3	75	24:5	82	32	92
17:1-14	68, 75	24:12	82	32:1	25, 64, 90
17:3	24	24:15	82	32:1-20	85, 90
17:4-11	75	24:16, 23	24	32:2	90
17:7	75	24:21	82	32:5	90
17:14	76	25:1	83	32:9	91
18:1-7	68, 76	25:1-12	82, 83	32:15-16	91

33:1	92	38:9-20	103	41:1-29	106, 110
33:1-24	85, 91	38:17	103	41:2	113
33:2	91	39	105	41:4	111
33:22	92	39:1	103	41:5-7	111
34-35	29	40	27, 28, 110,	41:8	111, 114,
34:1—35:10	30,		130, 154		126
	93	40-48	25, 30, 39,	41:9	112
34:1-2	93		117, 121	41:10	112
34:1-17	93	40-55	21	41:11-12	112
34:2	94, 95	40-66	19, 21, 24,	41:13	112
34:6	163		131	41:14	112
34:8	94	40:1	24, 66, 105,	41:15	113
35	27, 95, 113		128	41:16	113
35:1-10	93, 95	40:1—48:22	31,	41:17	113
35:8	24, 66, 95		105, 106	41:18	113
35:10	95, 128	40:1—66:24	28,	41:19	113
36-37	92		29, 31, 105	41:20	113
36-39	29, 97, 99	40:1-11	106	41:21	113, 127
36:1	18, 97, 98	40:1-31	106	41:22	113
36:1—37:38	99	40:2	106, 161	41:24	113
36:1—39:8	29, 30	40:3	24, 66, 95,	41:25	113
36:2	99		107	41:28-29	114
36:6	99	40:3-5	107	42	132
36:10	99	40:4-5	107	42:1	25, 114,
36:21	100	40:5	24, 38, 152		126
36:22	100	40:6-8	107	42:1-4	114
37	17, 24, 97	40:9-11	107	42:1-9	114
37:8	100	40:12	108	42:1-25	106
37:14	100	40:12-31	108	42:2	110, 115
37:15-20	101	40:13	108	42:4	132
37:19	101	40:15	108	42:6	115
37:31	24	40:18	108, 109	42:7	115
37:32	62	40:19	108	42:8	115
37:35	101	40:20	108	42:9	115
37:35-36	89	40:22	108	42:10	115
37:36	101	40:25	109	42:10-25	115
38:1	98, 101	40:26	109	42:29	114
38:1—39:8	101	40:27-31	109	43	26
38:2	102	40:28	109	43:1	116
38:5	102	40:31	109	43:1-28	106, 116
38:6	102	41:1	127	43:2	116

43:5	116	46:5-7	121	50:2	126
43:6	116	46:7	121	50:4	126
43:9	127	46:9-10	16	50:4-9	126
43:10	116	46:10-11	121	50:6	127, 132
43:11, 25	24	46:11	121	50:7	127
43:11-17	117	46:12	128	50:10	127
43:16	117	46:12-13	122	51:1	128
43:18-20	117	46:13	128	51:1-16	128
43:19	24	47	122	51:1-23	125, 127
43:21	117	47:1	122	51:2	128
43:24	117	47:1-15	106, 122	51:3	128
43:25	117	47:5	122	51:5	128
43:26	127, 162	47:10	122	51:9	129
44-45	30, 70	48	128	51:10	128
44:1-28	106, 117	48:1	123	51:11	96
44:2	117	48:1-22	106	51:12	24
44:3	117	48:4	23	51:17	129
44:6—45:25	16	48:8	123	51:17-21	162
44:6-8	117	48:12	123	51:17-23	128
44:9-20	118	48:14, 16	127	51:22	129
44:13-20	28	48:15	24	51:23	129
44:16-17	118	48:18	123	52:1-12	125, 129
44:21	118	48:20	124, 162	52:2	129
44:26	118	48:22	30, 105,	52:4	129
44:28	106, 111,		124, 149	52:5	129
	119, 118	49	114, 132	52:6	129
45:1	106, 111,	49-57	31, 105,	52:7	129
	119		106, 125, 131	52:8	129
45:1-8	119	49:1-13	125	52:9	130
45:1-25	106, 119	49:1-26	125	52:10	129
45:4	119, 120	49:3	126	52:11	130, 162
45:9-17	120	49:4	132	52:11-12	129
45:14	155	49:6	21, 126	52:12	130
45:17	120	49:11	24	52:13	132
45:18	20	49:14	126	52:13—53:12	125,
45:20	127	49:14-26	125		131
45:22	120	49:15-16	126	52:13-15	134, 135
45:23	120	49:26	126	52:15	135, 136
46:1-13	106, 120	50	128	53	38, 114, 133,
46:1-2	121	50:1-11	125, 126		142, 144
46:3	24, 121	50:1-3	126	53:1	128

53:1-3	134, 135, 136	56:9-12	147	61:2	25, 160, 164
53:2	25, 136	56:10	129	61:3	160
53:4	137	56:11	147	61:4-8	159
53:4-6	134, 135, 137	57:1	148	61:6	160
53:5	138, 139	57:1-21	125, 147	61:7	157, 161
53:5-6	138	57:5	148	61:9	161
53:6	25, 139, 147	57:14	24	61:10	161
53:7	140	57:15	148	62	156, 160
53:7-9	134, 135, 139	57:19	24	62:1-12	151, 161
53:10	25, 141	57:20-21	149	62:2	161
53:10-12	134, 140	57:21	30, 105, 124	62:3	161
53:11	141	58-66	31	62:5	162
53:13	135	58:1—66:24	31, 105, 151	62:6	162
53:13-15	135	58:1-14	151	62:7	162
54	27	58:3	152	62:9	162
54-57	142	58:9	152	62:10	24, 162, 163
54:1-17	125, 142	58:14	38, 152	62:12	163
54:2	143	59:1-21	151, 152	63	156, 157, 160
54:3	143	59:2	152	63:1-19	151, 163
54:5	143	59:16	153	63:2	163
54:7	144	59:20	153	63:3	25, 163
54:8	144	60:1-22	151, 153	63:4	164
54:9	144	60:2	154	63:5	164
54:11-17	144	60:3	154	63:7	164
54:17	144	60:4	154	63:9	165
55:1	66	60:5	154	63:11	165
55:1-13	125, 144	60:6	154	63:15	165
55:2-3	145	60:8	154	63:16	165
55:3	145	60:9	154	63:19	166
55:6	146	60:11	155	64-66	166
55:8	146	60:12	155	64:1	166
55:11	146	60:19	155	64:1-12	151, 166
56:1-12	125, 146	61	23, 115, 156, 159, 161	64:2	167
56:1-2	146	61-63	155	64:4	167
56:3	147	61:1	157, 158, 161	64:5	167
56:3-5	147			64:6	167
56:6	147	61:1-2	25	65	166
56:7	147	61:1-11	151, 155	65:1	168
				65:1-25	151, 168
				65:2	168

65:5 168
65:8-9 24
65:8-10 168
65:13-15 168
65:17 96, 169
65:20 169
65:25 170
66:1-24 151, 170
66:2 170
66:3 170
66:12 170
66:16 170

Jeremiah
1:1 15
6:17 129
12:12 113
18:6 167
23:5 43
25:1-11 122
31:31 145
33:15 43
46-51 67
51:51 127

Lamentations
2:1 155

Ezekiel
1:1-28 46
13 15
3:8-9 127
3:17 129
10:1-22 46
25-32 67
25:8-11 74
28:1-19 73
28 79
28:12-19 73
28:14, 17 73
31:9 128

33:2, 7 129
33:24 28
44:18 161
48:35 66, 155

Daniel
2:32, 35, 45 87
2:35 170
3:1-30 116
4:1-18 72
5 122
9 73
9:3-11 167
9:4-5 153
9:16 133
9:26 140
10:11 48
10:15-17 48

Hosea
1:1 18, 35
4:1-19 86
7:1 18
10:1 43
11:1 56
11:8 52

Joel
3:10 40
3:13 164

Amos
1:1 18, 35
6:1-14 86

Jonah
1:3 154
2:1-9 103

Micah
1:1 35

2:5-7 86
4 40

Habakkuk
1:5-11 94, 116
1:12—2:1 122
1:12—2:20 63
3:17-19 161

Haggai
2:16 164

Zechariah
3:8 43, 133
6:12 43
9:9 132, 133
10:1 155
12:10 132, 133, 136
13:7 132, 133
14:7 155
14:16 155

Malachi
4:2 153-54

NEW TESTAMENT
Matthew
1:1 62, 91
2 154
2:14-15 56
3:3 107
3:17 61, 158
4:1-11 102
4:13-16 59
4:14 26
5:4 160
5:6 145
7:13-14 127
8:5-13 137

8:17	26, 138	4:1-13	102	16:11	72
9:13	49	4:16-31	156	19:11	140
9:36	139	4:18-19	23, 25,	21:20	48
11:28-30	115		26		
12:17	26	4:20	158	Acts	
12:17-21	114	4:21	25	2:23	141
16:23	73	4:22	159	3:13	114
17:5	61	4:27	156	4:27	114
21:13	147	8:2-3	137	4:30	114
21:33-44	43	9:51	127	7:49-50	170
22:29	119	18	162	8:28	26
23:13-15	85	19:46	147	8:34	133
23:23	85			8:35	133
23:25	85	John		10:38	60
23:27	85	1:10-11	126, 137	13:32-34	145
23:29	85	1:14	57, 107	13:39	142
23:31	84	1:18	44, 46, 101	15:14	137
25:33-34	169	1:23	26, 107	17:24	46, 170
25:34	169	1:29	140	28:23	14
25:41	83	3:18	149	28:24-28	15
26:63-64	40	3:34	64, 157	28:25-27	27
26:67	127	3:36	149		
26:67-68	135	4:13-14	66	Romans	
27:27-30	135	4:14	46	1:3	62
27:30	127	4:24	118	1:20	47, 109
27:46	141	5:22	164	3	152
27:57	140	5:39-40	14	6:23	145
		6:26	137	8:17	81
Mark		6:37	145	8:19-22	47, 65
1:3	107	6:45	145	8:21	95, 164, 169
7:25-30	137	6:44	137	8:22	95
9:48	171	7:37	145	8:33-34	144
10:45	61	10:11	107, 139	9:21-24	167
11:17	147	10:18	139	9:33	87
14:61	140	10:33	158	10:15	129
14:62	140	10:35	98	10:16	27
		12:31	72	10:20	27
Luke		12:37-41	44-45	10:20-21	168
1:32-33	62	12:41	14, 26	11	117
2:13	143	14:30	72	11:1-6	131, 168
3:4-6	107	15:5	89	11:5	50

11:11-12	143-44	2:20	87	12:22-24	107
11:12	84	2:20-22	87	13:20-21	107, 139
11:15	143-44				
11:15	84	Philippians		James	
11:26	66	2:5-11	57	1:25-26	152
12:2	152	2:8-11	135	4:6	42
14:11	120	2:10-11	120		
15:12	27	4:4	161	1 Peter	
		4:7	41	1:10-12	25, 90
		4:13	109	1:11	31, 142, 156
1 Corinthians				1:24-25	107
2:9	167	Colossians		2:6	87
2:10	167	1:16	47	2:9	160
2:10-11	35	2:3	61	2:23	140
3:11	87			2:25	107, 139
4:3	41	1 Thessalonians		3:3-4	42
4:7	48	4:16-18	84	5:4	107, 139
8:4-6	101			5:5	42
10:12	104	2 Thessalonians		5:10	81
10:32	131	1	160		
15:3	139			2 Peter	
15:3-4	141	1 Timothy		1:16-18	107
15:25-26	169	3:6	74	1:19	73
15:47	96	5:23	138	1:20-21	35
15:54	83			1:21	16, 26
		2 Timothy		2:1	41
		3:16-17	35	3:9	122, 159
2 Corinthians		4:20	138		
4:4	72, 142			1 John	
4:6	153	Hebrews		1:1-2	107
5:7	166	1:1	16, 35, 126	1:9	49
5:21	139	1:2	126		
12:7-10	138	1:3	61	Revelation	
		2:10	141	1:4	20, 64
Galatians		7:26	135	1:7	107, 160
6:16	131	10:7	140	1:17	48
		10:16-18	145	3:1	64
		11:29	165	3:10	84
Ephesians		11:37	18	4:1—5:14	46
2:8-9	145	12:2	141	6:10	166
2:14	148	12:4	126	6:15-17	42

7:17	83	18:4-5	130	20	65
8:13	85	19	160, 164	21:4	83
12:1-12	84	19:11	160	21:25	155
12:4	73	19:13	164	22	155
12:9	73	19:15	64	22:16	73
14:19	164	19:16	96	22:17	66, 145

Moody Press, a ministry of the Moody Bible Institute, is designed for education, evangelization, and edification. If we may assist you in knowing more about Christ and the Christian life, please write us without obligation: Moody Press, c/o MLM, Chicago, Illinois 60610